Start Where You Are

Start Where You Are

Matching Your Strategy to Your Marketplace

William B. Rouse

Jossey-Bass Publishers • San Francisco

Substantial discounts on bulk quantities of Jossey-Bass books are available to corporations, professional associations, and other organizations. For details and discount information, contact the special sales department at Jossey-Bass Inc., Publishers (415) 433–1740; Fax (800) 605–2665.

For sales outside the United States, please contact your local Simon & Schuster International Office.

 Manufactured in the United States of America on Lyons Falls Pathfinder Tradebook. This paper is acid-free and 100 percent totally chlorine-free.

Library of Congress Cataloging-in-Publication Data

Rouse, William B.
 Start where you are : matching your strategy to your marketplace / William B. Rouse.
  p. cm. — (The Jossey-Bass management series)
 Includes bibliographical references (p.   ) and index.
 ISBN 0-7879-0247-0 (acid-free paper)
 1. Strategic planning. I. Title. II. Series.
HD30.28. R675 1996
658.4'012—dc20
                                                                95-47030
                                                                CIP

FIRST EDITION
HB Printing   10 9 8 7 6 5 4 3 2 1

The Jossey-Bass
Business & Management Series

Contents

Preface

Knowing where you are is the key to getting where you want to go. Thus, companies need to assess their current situations before developing strategic plans for pursuing their visions. They need to assess both their current and future relationships with their markets.

This book is designed to help you assess your company's situation. It presents a step-by-step methodology that builds upon a few primary concepts: *common business situations*, *key situation assessment questions*, and *indicators of current and future situations*. It explains how *transitions* lead to *patterns of situations* and how these constitute a company's *story*. Finally, it explains how awareness of these transitions and patterns can be used to help create the story you want to create.

The situation assessment methodology is intended to help you answer three important questions:

- What is my current relationship with the marketplace?
- What future relationships are possible and likely?
- How will my actions affect my future?

The book explains how to answer these questions and how to use the answers you get. In the process, it illustrates how change can and does happen. Old patterns of situations—or old stories—can be laid to rest. New stories can be created. Apparently inevitable transitions can be replaced with more desirable transitions. In the book, I define a set of methods and tools that I have put to the test in more than one hundred enterprises.

Background and Purpose

In my recent work I have explored the nature of planning in companies and other types of enterprises such as government agencies, universities, and nonprofit organizations. I have focused on what makes planning so difficult, what can be done to facilitate the planning process, and which organizational changes may help implement plans successfully.

I have found that many companies do not really plan. They do not think strategically. Rather, they extrapolate based on past events and budget for projected consequences. As a result, when the future is not a mere continuation of the past, they experience crisis.

Strategic thinking involves understanding trends and opportunities in the marketplace and a company's strengths and weaknesses in the face of these trends and opportunities. It involves understanding a company's current and possible future relationships with markets. For example, is it ahead of the market, in step with the market, or behind the market?

Strategic planning starts with strategic thinking and then translates what is learned into market-related goals, strategies, and plans. Goals involve sales, profits, market share, and so on. Strategies focus on providing benefits to customers in ways that create competitive advantages for a company and thereby attain the goals that are sought. Strategic plans outline—in broad terms at first and then in more detail—the steps that need to be taken to carry out the strategy. The plans are then translated into tactical and operational plans and finally into budgets.

Fortunately, I have seen many successful instances of this kind of planning. I have realized that two kinds of circumstances often serve as the catalyst for successful planning efforts.

A company that finds itself in the first kind of circumstance is facing fundamental changes in its markets or technologies. A good example of a changing market is the rapid decline in defense markets; an example of a changing technology is the accelerating shift from centralized to distributed computing. As a result, many companies in both the defense and computer industries are facing challenges. These companies have no choice but to respond.

The second kind of circumstance that precipitates planning involves opportunities. For example, increased environmental concerns and potential regulations may offer opportunities to companies that respond in creative and competitive ways. Similarly, new technologies such as the Internet and the World Wide Web offer opportunities to companies that can respond quickly and effectively. The prospects are compelling for companies attempting to respond to these opportunities, but they may have to undertake fundamental changes to do so.

My experiences with companies attempting to deal with change have led me to ask several questions. Why are some enterprises able to recognize the need to change, while many, if not most, are not? What kinds of change do enterprises think about? How do they implement change? And finally, how can enterprises anticipate, recognize, and respond to change?

I sought the answers to these questions through analysis of my experiences in such diverse industries as aerospace, automobiles, chemicals, communications, computers, defense, education, electronics, health care, semiconductors, steel, utilities, and others. My experiences yielded hundreds of case studies, yet it seemed none of them was unique. Intuitively, at least, I believed there had to be a small set of situations that are common to all businesses. By the term *situation* I refer to a company's relationship with its markets. For example, perhaps a company is a leader with products that everybody wants or perhaps it's a follower with lower-cost versions of leading products.

I also felt that there were typical patterns of business situations. For instance, a company might start out ahead of the market. Then the market and other companies would catch up. Finally, if the company did not create new offerings, the market would eventually pass it by. I realized that variations on this pattern constitute each company's individual story.

Noticing the patterns of situations that result in stories led me to identify the ten common situations that companies experience. I saw how companies typically deal with these situations and how their responses lead to success or failure.

Thus, my own experiences provided the starting point for identifying the situations, the patterns of situations, and the stories created. However, these case studies were insufficient for a deep understanding of the issues because the period of time involved was not adequate for tracking the evolution of each situational type—fundamental change seldom happens quickly.

Consequently, I complemented my personal experiences with a historical review. I explored the transportation industry from its beginnings in the early 1800s, the computing industry from what may be deemed its origins in the mid 1800s, and the modern defense industry from what may be considered its origin, World War I. This historical approach offered a rich chronicle of technological change and the many people who championed these changes.

The driving impetus for all of this work was my desire to create mechanisms that would allow enterprises to understand and profit from their understanding of fundamental patterns of business situations. This book presents the mechanisms I have developed in the form of a strategic situation assessment methodology. The methodology is described and illustrated in a manner intended to help managers and executives think strategically about where they are and, thus, gain the key to going where they want to go.

Overview

This book deals with situation assessment in three sections. Part One focuses on providing the methods and tools for knowing where you are. The situation assessment methodology serves as a strong foundation for the deeper perspective presented in Part Two, in which a wide range of business stories are discussed. The last chapter of the book emphasizes creating your own business story.

Part One contains Chapters One through Four. It presents and illustrates the strategic situation assessment methodology. Chapter One describes the nature of patterns of business situations. These patterns involve transitions between different relationships with markets.

Chapter Two introduces the concept of the ten common situations. These common situations are the building blocks of all the business patterns. I call these ten situations *vision quest, evolution, crossover, crossing the chasm, steady growth, consolidation, silent war, paradigm lost, commodity trap*, and *process*. The chapter presents examples of each situation based both on my own experiences and on case studies.

Chapter Three considers the concept of business stories. Stories, as already noted, are created through the patterns of transitions between situations. Five typical stories are discussed. These are *classic life cycle, false start, death spiral, reinventing the company*, and *branching and pruning*. The chapter also discusses the perspective that companies usually bring with them to deal with change, limits to abilities to change, and correlates of successful change.

Chapter Four details the strategic situation assessment methodology. The step-by-step process relies on identification of the common situations, analysis of key situation assessment questions, and examination of indicators of current and potential situations. Examples illustrate how the methodology has been employed in both small, growing companies and large, mature companies.

Part Two—Chapters Five through Seven—provides a deeper perspective on patterns of change, focusing on the transportation, computer, and defense industries, respectively. Through the histories of these industries, a large number of enterprises are chronicled. These chapters describe more than a hundred companies that have made transitions between the common situations and, thereby, created their own stories.

The final chapter—Chapter Eight—discusses how you can create your own story. It emphasizes the need for ongoing situation assessment and considers limits on the ability to adapt. Finally, it examines the role of leadership. The focus in this concluding chapter—as in the rest of the book—is on creating the kind of mind-set that will allow managers and executives to identify and pursue opportunities in the midst of potential crises.

Acknowledgments

I have the good fortune to work with a number of the world's most admired enterprises. Many of these companies are very large. Many others are fairly small. Working with thousands of executives and senior managers in these enterprises has been and continues to be a tremendous learning experience. I could not have written this book without the opportunities that these firms and individuals have given me, and I gratefully acknowledge their help.

Atlanta, Georgia   William B. Rouse
January 1996

The Author

William B. Rouse is chief executive officer of Enterprise Support Systems, a business software publishing company headquartered in Atlanta. He has served in leadership roles on the faculties of Georgia Institute of Technology, Atlanta, and the University of Illinois, Urbana-Champaign. He also has served in visiting positions on the faculties of Delft University of Technology, the Netherlands, and Tufts University, Medford, Massachusetts. He received his B.S. from the University of Rhode Island and his S.M. and Ph.D. from the Massachusetts Institute of Technology.

Rouse has almost thirty years of experience in engineering, management, and marketing of information systems, decision support systems, and advanced training technology for complex vehicle, process, and organizational systems. His theoretical and applied contributions in these areas involve understanding and supporting human decision making and problem solving as well as human-computer interaction and information system design. Within these areas, he has written hundreds of technical articles and reports and has authored many books. Most recent among these books are *Best Laid Plans* (1994), *Catalysts for Change* (1993), *Strategies for Innovation* (1992), and *Design for Success* (1991). He currently serves as editor of the series *Human/Technology Interaction in Complex Systems*, published by JAI Press.

Rouse is a member of the National Academy of Engineering, a fellow of the Institute of Electrical and Electronics Engineers (IEEE), a fellow of the Human Factors and Ergonomics Society, and a senior member of the Institute of Industrial Engineers. He has received the Norbert Wiener Award from the IEEE Systems, Man, and Cybernetics Society, a Centennial Medal from IEEE, and the O. Hugo Schuck Award from the American Automation Control Council. He is listed in *Who's Who in America*, *Who's Who in Engineering*, and other biographical literature.

1

Finding the Pattern

Your Company's Evolving Relationship with the Market

Achieving success in business is not as simple as we would like it to be. Nevertheless, we all have a tendency to seek the silver bullet, to look for the one solution that will prove to be a panacea for all our business problems. Most recently, the business world has embraced continuous quality improvement and business process reengineering as likely silver bullets. These concepts are valuable and can help companies offer higher-quality and lower-cost products and services. However, nothing about them guarantees that the market will continue *to want* the products and services being offered.

Far more important for a company's success are its relationships with its markets. How can they be fostered and maintained? How can they be changed when necessary or desirable? Relationships with markets should be the central strategic concern of all businesses. Strategic thinking about these relationships is not simple—once again there are no silver bullets. However, this thinking can be done systematically.

This book provides a methodology for strategic thinking. Its goal is to help you assess your relationships—both current and potential—with your markets. It explains how these assessments can be used to improve your business strategies and plans. In other words, it shows you how to *start where you are in order to get to where you want to go*.

There are three key aspects to developing and implementing business strategies and plans:

1. *Assess the situation.* Situation assessment means understanding current and potential market situations and current and potential relationships with the market.

2. *Plan and commit.* Planning and commitment means developing appropriate strategic and tactical plans and committing the necessary resources to these plans.

3. *Execute and monitor.* Executing plans requires efficient and effective processes. Monitoring these processes is needed to assure that they yield high-quality, low-cost products and services.

Much attention is paid today to execution and monitoring, with substantial emphasis on tactical and, especially, operational plans. The already-mentioned emphasis on total quality management and business process reengineering provides ample evidence of this. Many people seem to think that value can be created by focusing solely on cutting costs. But they're wrong—it can't.

Increasing attention is also being devoted to planning and commitment in business strategies, as evidenced by a steady stream of business books that espouse strategic concepts and principles. For many companies, however, strategy and strategic thinking are elusive concepts. The here-and-now tends to dominate all their activities. Consequently, broad and sustained commitment to strategic planning is often very difficult to achieve.

The third leg of the business success stool—situation assessment—receives little attention. Many businesspeople do not seem to realize that they cannot get where they want to go unless they first know where they are. This book presents a straightforward methodology for assessing both current and future situations.

My premise is actually far from novel. I presume that evolving business situations create patterns. That is, I presume that companies' relationships with their markets create patterns. Understanding these patterns can provide the basis for substantial competitive advantage because it can enable a business to anticipate, recognize, and respond to changes much more quickly and effectively than its competitors do. My goal in this book is to provide readers with this understanding and the means for applying it to their advantage.

Patterns of Business Situations

Patterns of business situations operate within two contexts. At the macro level there are the overall economy and the industry within which a company operates; all companies must compete within this context, and it cannot be controlled. The micro level concerns an enterprise or a business unit within a larger enterprise. This level encompasses the things over which a company has some degree of control, such as market offerings, sales strategies, and organizational structures.

This book focuses on strategic situation assessment at the micro level but puts it in the context of the macro level. For example, it examines how a software company can assess its relationships with its markets in the context of trends and events in the software industry as well as in the economy in general. The focus is on helping this software company think strategically about its relationship with its markets.

The conceptual bases of the approach presented in this book are the following: *common business situations*, *key situation assessment questions*, and *indicators of current and future situations*. As you will see, the situation assessment methodology is concrete and specific. Before I present it, however, it is important to set the stage by discussing the three broad business situations that many—probably most—companies encounter.

A successful company often begins by being ahead of the market. Then the market catches up. In many cases, the market then passes the company by. When the market passes a company by, it is usually because there are mismatches between the company's presumptions—often implicit—about its situation and its actual situation. When and if these mismatches are identified, a company usually responds by trying to establish new relationships with its markets. The likelihood of such efforts succeeding is highly correlated with the company's ability to change itself too.

The Company Is Ahead of the Market

Most new ideas and new technologies are ahead of the market, often focusing on satisfying needs that people do not yet realize they have. Many technologies require a long maturation period until a large number of people are comfortable with them. Consequently, rather than pursuing existing markets, it is often necessary for businesses to create new markets for its ideas and technologies.

In such cases, business success depends on market innovations that inherently create change. Many market innovations have resulted from entrepreneurs anticipating customers' needs and becoming agents of change. For example, William Burroughs anticipated the calculator market. Henry Ford envisioned a car for every home. Steve Jobs and Steve Wozniak anticipated the personal computer market.

Such success stories seldom happen quickly. Innovative products are often greeted with little interest or even a negative reaction. For instance, in the late 1800s, typewriters, calculators, tabulators, and cash registers all encountered consumer resistance. It took about a hundred years for these four separate inventions to converge in the computer market; before that happened each one took a long time to be accepted in the market on its own.

In order to understand why a product or service is successful or unsuccessful, a company must understand what the market really needs and wants. Innovators often make the mistake of assuming that many people will inherently want their products and services. But in fact people want the *benefits* of the product or service, not the items themselves. Further complicating the situation, the benefits of products or services may only be understood by consumers when they are combined with other products or services to provide a total solution to their problem.

A historical example provides a good illustration. In the late 1800s and early 1900s the Fall River Line steamboats competed quite successfully with the railroads for passenger traffic between Boston and New York by offering a total package of transportation, lodging, and food. If the steamboats had tried to compete solely on speed of travel they would have failed miserably. But the company understood that business travelers needed a total solution to their travel problems, not just transportation. It recognized that travelers needed meals, a place to sleep, even entertainment. The Fall River Line steamboats provided all of this with their elegant overnight boat trips.

Thus, being ahead of the market means not only educating the audience and marketing the product in order to create a need for it but also gaining an understanding of consumers' overall problem and packaging the product to solve it. Achieving this goal may require extending a software product, for instance, or bundling it with other products and services. It is up to you to close the distance between yourself and your market.

The Market Catches Up

Of the many ideas and technologies that emerge, a few eventually do succeed. The products and services are created and at least a few customers buy them. Over time, the companies learn how to design and manufacture them in a way that meets the needs of a wider range of consumers. They learn how to market and sell the products and services most effectively. Once a product or service has achieved a certain level of market penetration—and this is usually a lengthy process—many new ventures are likely to be formed. Everyone wants to get into the software business today, for example. But only a few will achieve lasting success.

Again with the historical view, twenty-five hundred railroad companies had formed in the United States by the 1850s but in 1900 only thirty still survived. A large number of automobile companies were formed around the turn of the century but today only a few remain. A large number of aircraft companies were formed in the 1920s to 1940s but only a handful have survived.

Why did so many companies not survive? Their demise was not caused by a lack of motivation to succeed. It was not caused by a lack of investment. Instead, it was caused by their inadequate or incomplete understanding of markets—more specifically, their inadequate understanding of their current or emerging *relationships* with their markets. Consequently, they did not recognize the business risks associated with their current relationships and the business opportunities that others could make possible.

Thus, most new ventures disappear. They fail outright or they are acquired by the remaining participants in the market. Consolidation is a particular focus in this book. I examine why consolidation occurs and how a business can anticipate, recognize, and respond to the forces of consolidation. I explore how the ability to change—to make a successful transition from one situation to another—can result in the achievement of substantial success in consolidating markets. Success may mean being acquired for a handsome return, or it may mean acquiring and growing to become a dominant player in the market.

The Market Passes By

Achieving a dominant role is quite an accomplishment. However, it is not a tenured position. One need only look at past compilations of the Fortune 100 or the list of Dow Jones companies to see how many major players have passed from the scene. Why do these giants get into difficulties?

A primary source of difficulty is the inability to "read" the marketplace and the likely implications of trends. Thus U.S. aircraft engine manufacturers, overconfident because of their lead in piston engines, almost missed the jet engine. General Motors (GM) and Ford Motor Company missed the emerging small car market. Remington-Rand's lack of commitment gave the computer market to International Business Machines (IBM). But IBM missed the minicomputer market and Digital Equipment Corporation (DEC) missed the personal computer market. Dominant players regularly miss very important opportunities despite abundant talent and resources.

What are companies occupied with when opportunity knocks? In my experience, they are focused on dealing with today's issues and product lines. The noise level is so high that they cannot hear tomorrow knocking. The short term excludes the long term.

The odd thing about this is that companies probably should be focused on the short term, at least from the point of view of the overall economy. Individual enterprises become very good at doing X, and everybody benefits. When X is no longer relevant and Y is needed, these enterprises try to adapt but usually fade away instead. Meanwhile, new enterprises emerge to specialize in Y. Although this Darwinian process works well for the economy, many jobs are lost and lives disrupted along the way. Furthermore, from the point of view of the individual enterprise, this sequence of events is not acceptable. It wants to do well at X while also anticipating Y. But is this possible? Won't attention to Y undermine the focus on X? And why try to squeeze the last ounce out of X when you know that Y will eventually replace it?

These very difficult questions are central to an enterprise's ability to change itself in fundamental ways. In other words, must an enterprise accept the likely transitions between situations that past experience seems to dictate? Or can an enterprise creatively pursue and succeed with unlikely transitions? Success is certainly possible. It depends, however, on understanding the situation being experienced and the ways in which alternative futures can be created.

Mismatches in Situation Assessments

When the market gets ahead of a company, it is usually because that company's assessment of its situation is mismatched with the actual situation. For example, you think that your new software product, which offers higher quality and lower price, will put you back on the path of steady growth. But, in fact, multimedia products are poised to take over the market because of their high storage capacity and great visual appeal. Indeed, that upstart company you discounted a few years ago is about to take away your customers.

Mismatches such as these, if not remediated, are likely to result in the disintegration of a company's relationships with its markets. Unfortunately, many companies fail to recognize the possibility of such disintegration early enough to be able to respond effectively. By the time they realize that multimedia is the future, they have already invested all their capital in other technologies.

I have repeatedly observed the following scenario in the computer and defense industries. A mismatch between a company's assumed and actual relationship with the marketplace precipitates a crisis. Perhaps the company thinks that it is in a steady growth situation when in fact new technologies have undermined that possibility. In reality, the company's mainframe software products are in deep trouble because customers are increasingly adopting a distributed computing paradigm.

Rarely do such crises arise because companies fail to adapt to a new situation. Rather, they arise because companies seldom perceive that the new situation exists. Instead, they focus on tactical or operational issues such as quality improvement or process reengineering. Thus, they try to be the highest-quality, lowest-cost producers of a soon-to-be obsolete product or service!

The crisis continues. The focus turns increasingly inward. Stories of past successes are revisited. In retelling these stories, the company rather than the marketplace is usually emphasized. For example, discussions are likely to focus on the primacy of core competencies, independent of market needs. As the company becomes increasingly preoccupied with this self-centered story, it further loses track of the marketplace. Basically, a company caught in this scenario is trying to make its old "story" work while ignoring a fundamental mismatch with the current and future marketplace. GM's reluctance and delay in adapting to market changes in the 1980s and 1990s provides an excellent example of this phenomenon.

This is the scenario that unfolds in many of the case studies presented in this book. Failure to understand the necessity of making the transition from one situation to the next results in an inward focus that exacerbates the crisis. Once the crisis becomes overwhelming, top management may realize the predicament. But realization at this point is too late. Fortunately, this fate is not inevitable.

Changing Relationships and Organizations

For a company to deal with the forces outlined thus far it must be able to consider making substantial organizational changes. Many enterprises attempt to make major changes in their external market image while also trying to minimize the internal changes they make to themselves. In other words, they attempt to create a new relationship with the marketplace—a new situation—while maintaining the old internal values, structures, and roles with few if any modifications.

This attempt seldom if ever works. Enterprises in transition almost always have to redesign themselves. Unfortunately, doing this is very difficult. Because of a variety of subtle yet substantial forces, the result is often inefficient and ineffective response to change.

One important force to overcome is fear of change. I have found that people who are good at optimizing within a given paradigm—producing the lowest-cost, highest-quality X—are not necessarily good at changing paradigms and producing Y. A good example of this behavior is that of Thomas Watson, Sr., CEO of IBM, who clung to punch cards—a product that he had not invented but had perfected—rather than recognize the improvements that magnetic tape made possible. Another example is Ken Olsen, CEO of DEC, who refused to outsource production of any elements of DEC computers. Apple Computer's refusal until recently to adopt an open architecture for its computers provides yet another example of this attitude.

It is quite possible for leaders who excel in one situation to have difficulties with others. Some leaders are better at creating visionary new products and growing the markets for these products. Others are better in consolidation situations where cost cutting and close scrutiny of financial performance are central issues. Thus, quite often leaders, or at least leadership styles, need to be matched to situations.

Another significant problem to overcome can be the great difficulty involved in changing an enterprise's culture. Culture may be very subtle—until you attempt to change it. Then you may be quite surprised to find that it is very strong indeed, that its story, as I call it, is very deeply ingrained.

Quite often the company's story and the culture it creates are likely to have been nurtured inadvertently. For example, many companies in the defense industry have a technology-driven culture that grew without conscious intent out of almost total reliance on relationships with the Department of Defense. Transforming such cultures into more market-driven ones is a difficult task.

Yet another barrier to overcome is the grieving for the "good old days," which have a tendency to get better as they grow more removed from the present. The old story is retold and relished. Substantial energy and emotion are devoted wistfully to recalling simpler times when customer demands were easy to meet and competitors were few. As a result, new customers—and the new story—are viewed as second best.

Clearly, change is tough. The forces in enterprises uphold stable optimization within the dominant paradigm of the old story. Complete belief in the old paradigm and story strongly influences the hypotheses considered, the information sought, the knowledge gained. A variety of vested interests quite understandably conspire to maintain and enhance the status quo.

Yet change can and does happen. Old stories can be laid to rest and new stories created. The old inevitable transitions between situations can be replaced by more desirable transitions.

Situation Assessment

Situation assessment means determining the nature of a company's relationships with its markets. For example, are you a leader with products that everybody wants or a follower with lower cost versions of leading products? To make this determination, you must be aware of both your current relationships and your potential relationships. You must also be aware of the overall business trends in these markets.

The methodology that I discuss in this book will enable you to assess your company's situation. It is a three-step methodology:

1. Compare marketplace signals and situation indicators in order to determine likely current and future situations. The basis for this comparison is a set of common situations.
2. Consider the consequences of these situations. To do this, draw upon the typical implications of the common situations.
3. Finally, evaluate the desirability of these consequences and the resources needed to pursue these situations.

This book explains how to use this methodology to develop strategies and plans that will help you avoid undesirable future situations and create desirable ones. Of particular importance, it will teach you how to think strategically about your relationships with your markets.

Here's an illustration. Let's assume you are in the consumer electronics business. If you are a typical executive or senior manager today, you are probably in the midst of reengineering. You are trying to streamline processes and cut costs, just as a few years ago— having adopted total quality concepts—you were trying to measure and improve the quality of your processes.

But the utility of investing in improvements and cutting costs depends on the effectiveness of your business strategy. In other words, you too may be on the path to high-quality, low-cost products that are rapidly becoming obsolete. You need a strategy for growth that will enable you to adapt to changes in the dynamic consumer electronics market.

There is a great natural temptation to choose quickly from a variety of standard strategies. For example, if you were in this situation you might pursue high-volume cost leadership in the full breadth of the consumer electronics market. Or you might focus on the high end of the market with unique functions and features that enable premium prices for your products. Finally, you might focus on specialized niches where customized products can command high prices.

Consideration of these three alternatives and many detailed variations of them requires careful analyses of potential revenues and costs associated with each. Strategic planning often quickly turns to such analyses, and this is usually where strategic thinking ends.

But successful strategic thinking begins long before this process: it begins with situation assessment. The purpose of situation assessment is to answer the following questions: What are my current relationships with my markets? What future relationships are possible and likely? How will my actions affect my future?

As already noted, situation assessment focuses on relationships with markets. What are your assumptions about your relationships with the consumer electronics market, both now and in the future? If you have thought about this question at all, my guess is that you have assumed that your relationship with this marketplace will continue as it has been. Perhaps this is your implicit assumption. Whether explicit or implicit, this assumption is most likely wrong!

Relationships with markets are very seldom static. We assume that they are static and we act as if they are static. But in fact these relationships wax and wane. They have ups and downs. The ups happen when we are in tune with our markets. The downs happen when we are out of tune with them, usually because the tune has changed.

Fortunately, as discussed earlier, such changes follow patterns. The patterns are made up of business situations and transitions between them. The ten common situations are the following: *vision quest, evolution, crossover, crossing the chasm, steady growth, consolidation, silent war, paradigm lost, commodity trap,* and *process.* Although detailed discussion of the common situations will wait until the next chapter, it will be useful to preview here the kinds of questions that one asks during a situation assessment.

The Assessment Methodology

The situation assessment methodology intends to provide the answers to questions about relationships with your markets. To do this, it phrases the questions in the following three broad categories:

1. What is the situation?

2. How is the situation likely to unfold?

3. Which situation should be pursued?

To answer these questions, it is necessary to refer to the ten common situations. To help you decide which ones are affecting your company, this book provides a set of indicators whose presence or absence correlate with situations. These attributes serve as present indicators of current situations and as leading indicators of future situations. Use of the common situations and indicators brings structure and rigor to the situation assessment process.

This structure and rigor can be invaluable when a company entertains substantial change. While initially there is a natural tendency to avoid change, there often emerges a strong inclination to "get on with it" and make decisions and changes quickly. For example, when a company senses that the market has passed it by, it may quickly decide to acquire one or more small companies that have leading-edge technologies relevant to that market. Top management may feel that these acquisitions have solved their problems. However, they still may not have addressed the fundamental nature of their relationship with their market. Consequently, the acquisitions may in fact have created new problems. The situation assessment method discussed in this book supports more prudent decision making in dealing with change.

To answer the question "What is the situation?" you compare marketplace signals and situation indicators to determine your probable current and future situations. Doing this usually results in multiple possibilities, particularly for the future. It is good to have multiple alternatives at this point because subsequent questions are likely to make one or more of them unattractive.

To answer the question "How is the situation likely to unfold?" you consider the implications of the likely situations by drawing upon a compilation of the typical implications presented in Chapter Two. Doing this allows for projecting likely consequences of potential situations. Thinking about these consequences usually involves going from the general to the specific for your company.

To answer the question "Which situation should be pursued?" you evaluate the desirability of these consequences as well as the resources required for each. These evaluations mutually influence the choice of opportunities to pursue. At this point, the number of alternatives usually becomes quite constrained, often limited to only one or two opportunities.

Situation Assessment and Strategic Planning

It is important to put the situation assessment methodology in perspective. It is much less an alternative methodology for strategic planning than a complementary methodology that should be employed as the first phase of the planning process. In this manner, it provides value in ways that strengthen subsequent use of any strategic planning approach.

As already noted, a central tenet of this methodology is that businesses evolve through patterns of situations or relationships with their markets. Each company's pattern constitutes its story. When a company's ability to understand and affect its patterns is improved, it is empowered to avoid undesirable patterns and create the story it envisions.

This story-based view is certainly not new. Case study has long been a staple of business schools. The use of scenarios in business planning is common, too, as is another notion presented in this book, that of a business having a "mental model" of the ways in which it interacts with the marketplace.

Peter Schwartz's work, summarized in *The Art of the Long View* (1991), is an excellent illustration of the use of scenario planning. Schwartz outlines a systematic process for developing scenarios. The process begins by identifying a focal issue or decision. Then the key forces in the environment affecting or potentially affecting this issue or decision are listed; from these, the driving forces are determined. Next, the key forces and trends are ranked by importance and level of certainty. Based on this information, scenarios are developed, usually one that is optimistic, one that is pessimistic, and one that falls in between. The scenarios are then fleshed out and the implications of each determined. Finally, leading indicators are selected to help management ascertain which scenario is unfolding as time goes on.

Peter Drucker's notion of the "theory of a business" resembles the situation assessment methodology's use of the mental model concept. In his article "The Theory of the Business" (*Harvard Business Review*, 1994), Drucker argues that a primary reason why many mature companies encounter substantial difficulties with change is that their theories of the business are no longer working. In other words, the implicit assumptions—concerning society, markets, customers, and technologies—upon which the enterprises are premised and managed no longer match the reality of their relationships with the marketplace.

Schwartz's scenarios and Drucker's theories both suggest a need to explore appropriate premises or assumptions before beginning strategic planning. The approach I present in this book merely goes a step further, providing a methodology for doing so. Thus, Drucker's notion of a theory of the business is operationalized in a way that sets the stage for Schwartz's approach to scenario planning.

A Value-Added Methodology

The situation assessment methodology presented in this book has four main advantages.

First, it offers a set of common business situations—introduced in the next chapter—for you to build on as you consider your current situation and likely future situations. Thus, you do not have to theorize about your situation on your own.

Second, it explains the common patterns of transitions between these situations. Common patterns are not preordained. However, in my experience, unless a business is aware of these patterns, it is very unlikely to avoid them.

Third, the book offers a set of common indicators to help you recognize current or future situations. This knowledge can help you track and predict your situation or relationships with the marketplace. Doing this will help you to anticipate, recognize, and respond to changes at both the macro and micro levels.

Finally, this methodology provides a strong foundation upon which to base other approaches. Situation assessments provide strong assumptions upon which scenarios can be constructed.

In sum, the situation assessment methodology laid out in this book should serve as an important "front end" for strategic planning. Creating and maintaining an accurate assessment of a company's relationships with its markets are central to developing relevant and useful strategic plans. In other words, *knowing where you are is a key to getting where you want to go*.

Range of Applicability

The book presents a large number of vignettes and case studies that are based on my personal experiences with many enterprises as well as on extensive historical research. The stories of more than a hundred enterprises are related. Many began in the early 1800s and quite a few of them are still being played out today.

These stories chronicle the emergence, growth, and maturity of the transportation, computer, and defense industries. They tell of

steamboats, railroads, automobiles, airplanes, typewriters, calculators, tabulators, cash registers, and others. You will learn how enterprises have dealt with changing relationships with their markets.
This look at the fascinating panorama created by the historical and
the contemporary business world will help you gain a solid perspective with which to gauge your own situation. And of greatest importance, you will learn how to anticipate, recognize, and respond to
the forces of change that either affect or may soon affect both you
and your enterprise.

2

Identifying Where You Are

The Ten Most Common Situations

The process of starting four small companies and working with well over a hundred other companies has led me to the conclusion that most companies have much in common. Companies are born. They crawl and stumble. Some grow and mature. And eventually, most decline.

The Elements of Business Patterns

During the process of birth, growth, maturity, and decline, most enterprises share many experiences. Their stories follow similar patterns. The elements of these patterns are the ten common situations. These situations capture the essence of companies' relationships with their markets as they grow, mature, decline, and sometimes rejuvenate themselves.

The ten common situations cover a range of relationships with the marketplace:

- *Vision quest* and *evolution* situations occur when a company attempts to create relationships with the market and when those relationships are emerging.

- *Crossover* and *crossing the chasm* situations occur when a company cultivates narrow relationships and then attempts to broaden them.

- *Steady growth* and *consolidation* situations occur when the company has broad relationships, initially with it dominating and later with the marketplace dominating.

- *Silent war* and *paradigm lost* occur when relationships with the marketplace become increasingly tenuous.

- *Commodity trap* and *process* situations occur when the marketplace is firmly in charge.

This chapter explains the situations themselves in detail and summarizes their indicators and implications. Exhibit 2.1 summarizes the discussion of this chapter. Indicators and implications for each of the ten common situations are noted. The ways in which these changing situations can and should affect a business's strategic thinking are discussed in Chapter Three.

I hasten to note that not all companies experience all of these situations. In fact, everyone's goal should be to pursue the more desirable situations and avoid the less desirable ones.

Vision Quest

Let's say you have an idea for a new software product, a new tool for travel planning. Your CD-ROM will allow users to view routes, parks, attractions, hotels, restaurants, and so on. Through the use of networks, they will make reservations, pay for their reservations, and manage their trip budgets online. Thus, your product will enable customers to do something they have always wanted to do— efficiently and effectively maximize their travel opportunities while sticking to their budgets. You understand how to make this new software work. You are determined to make it work, no matter what. You head out to the garage. You are on a *vision quest*.

Many companies have emerged and quite a few have changed directions based on one or more individuals' compelling vision of a market need or emerging market need. Such individuals also usually have a strong sense of how they can satisfy that need.

EXHIBIT 2.1. The Ten Common Situations and Their Indicators and Implications.

Situation	Indicators	Implications
Vision quest	Missionary zeal of champions who have strong commitment despite mixed signals from marketplace. Feedback indicates that product is ahead of the times.	Can be good, but make sure that you want to be in this situation. Try to learn how to recast vision in market-oriented terms. Avoid proliferation of visions. Gain top management commitment, the sooner the better.
Evolution	There is continual missing of development targets and/or sales targets. Compatibility problems with existing infrastructure, marketplace skepticism, and perceptions of risk are also present.	Patience with progress may be necessary. Continual reselling to top management and investors is likely to be required. Other sources of cash flow may be needed.
Crossover	Necessary or desired market innovations are not possible without importing technologies or processes. Limited number of key technologies or processes are applicable in domains other than where they originated. Targeted domains are unaware of applicability of technologies or processes.	You can gain substantial competitive advantage if you are right. Avoid tendency to carry over too much; avoid burdening crossover technologies or processes with elements of original domain that are not useful in new domain.

EXHIBIT 2.1. (cont.)

Situation	Indicators	Implications
Crossing the chasm	Sales thus far are limited to innovators and early adopters. You have difficulty articulating benefits of your product to pure pragmatists and difficulty packaging as part of whole product solution.	Shift emphasis from intriguing inventions to compelling problems solved and concrete value added. Packaging of products and services, as well as marketing and sales, must be totally market driven in terms of the concerns, values, and perceptions of the pragmatic majority.
Steady growth	There are steadily growing sales, perhaps market share and profits; increased market acceptance of technologies; clear progress up production learning curve.	A great place to be—you've made it!—but very few enterprises are able to stay in this situation. Anticipating transitions to other situations can enable changing and thereby avoiding transitions or at least expediting them.

EXHIBIT 2.1. (cont.)

Situation	Indicators	Implications
Consolidation	An increasing number of players are all scrambling for market share. Pressure to lower prices comes at the same time that the costs of marketing and sales increase. Margins are rapidly eroding. Few discretionary resources are available to invest in gaining competitive advantage.	Number of players usually decreases dramatically as many fold or are acquired. You should cash in to gain capital for other ventures or be prepared to spend to acquire market share. Those who survive can do quite well, although substantial long-term debt may be incurred.
Silent war	Potential new players are nibbling at heels of major players. Relevant new technologies are appearing in technical literature, starting with science publications and then with engineering publications. New technologies are maturing in other domains.	You need to recognize potential war as soon as possible. You might form new ventures to nibble at your own heels. You need to pursue aggressively new technologies with R&D, consortia, alliances, or acquisitions to assure continued competitive advantage.

EXHIBIT 2.1. (cont.)

Situation	Indicators	Implications
Paradigm lost	Dominant technologies or processes underlying your products are becoming less central in other domains. Your technologies or processes are unable to meet market expectations for performance, quality, and cost. New and growing players in your markets do not employ improved versions of your technologies or processes.	There are substantial risks of ceasing to be a major player or a player at all. It is late to catch up with R&D or consortia; alliances or acquisitions likely to be necessary. You may withdraw from affected market segments.
Commodity trap	Everybody is selling the same thing; quality, service, and price are all that matters. Costs of marketing and sales are high. Deep discounts are necessary; gross and net margins are low.	Can be terrible and usually is. However, there are possibilities to transition to a steady growth situation, which is most likely if process situation is pursued quickly.
Process	Product innovations are of less value because de facto or actual industry standards have emerged. There are pressures to decrease costs of goods sold as well as costs of sales as percent of sales. Financial ratios are worse than industry averages.	Competitive advantages have to be gained through process improvements. Shift from product to process orientation is needed. Recognize and improve processes that previously went unnoticed, that is, marketing and sales, product support, and so on.

Those who "own" the vision can be characterized as determined to succeed regardless of hurdles and hindrances.

The first hurdle is often the market's reluctance to have the need satisfied. Often the market is not aware of the need. In other cases, although the need is evident this solution is not compelling. It is considered too new, too risky, and frequently too expensive. Thus, while a relationship with the marketplace is the goal when one is on a vision quest, initially the relationship is just not there.

Nevertheless, people on vision quests tend to persist. Years, sometimes decades, pass. For the fortunate few, the visions are eventually realized. Far many more visionaries never see their visions realized, at least not in terms of business success.

We encounter many vision quest situations in the chronicles and case histories described in Chapters Five through Seven. Henry Ford envisioned a mass market for automobiles and in his ninth attempt finally succeeded in creating one. Alfred Sloan envisioned professional management in the automobile industry. Realization of his vision led to great success for General Motors. It has been argued, however, that the institution created by Sloan is that company's biggest problem today. Thus, a vision may turn out to be both positive and negative.

The aviation industry has been the backdrop for many vision quests. Jack Northrop's vision of a flying wing and Igor Sikorsky's vision of a helicopter are two of the more notable ones. Both took many years—in fact, many decades—before they were realized.

In the computer industry, vision quests include that of Burroughs and calculators, of Hollerith and punched-card tabulators, of Olsen and interactive computing, of Englebart and graphical user interfaces, of Nelson and hypertext, of Kay and notebook computers, and of Sculley and personal digital assistants. All of these visions were seen as ideas that were very much ahead of their times. Success in the market usually was not as great as expected or took much longer than originally anticipated.

The vision quest is a particularly interesting phenomenon because it illustrates the effects that people can have on their times as opposed to the effects their times have on them. This is because a vision quest proceeds even when the times are not ready for it. Patience, persistence, and often passion drive visionaries to overcome obstacles and sometimes to succeed. Although the vision quest may seem to be a positive situation— even an uplifting one—it also has drawbacks. The result of a vision quest may be decades of business failure before success finally is achieved. Indeed, the wait can be too long, resulting in paradigm lost situations (described later in this chapter), which visionaries usually fail to see until it is too late.

Indications of a vision quest situation include missionary zeal and a strong commitment to the vision. These feelings are likely to be strong despite mixed signals from the marketplace. Those who have not accepted the vision are likely to wonder why the commitment continues despite such poor results. A common message from the marketplace is that the product is ahead of the market. Potential investors and customers are likely to focus on what they perceive to be immature technology. Consequently, they see only high risks.

The individuals involved in a vision quest have to make sure that they have the patience, persistence, and passion necessary to sustain it. To increase the possibilities for realizing their vision, they should try to recast it in market-oriented terms. They should focus on benefits provided—problems solved—rather than on novelty and innovation. Specifically, success depends on translating one's fascination with particular technologies into tangible benefits for the marketplace. In this way, the visionary and the market may eventually share the same vision.

It is also important to avoid proliferating visions. Vision quests consume a lot of energy. If the energy is spread among many, it is likely that none will succeed. Most important is the energy and commitment of top management, which will eventually be essential for success. The sooner top management internalizes the quest, the better.

Evolution

You have been developing your software product for quite some time now. It works pretty well, most of the time. Sometimes it is rather slow, even painfully slow. But you have sold two. Your neighbor bought one. A "real customer" bought another. Both have been giving you lots of great ideas for ways to improve your product. Often you get the feeling your travel planning tool will soon take off; then you realize that it is not yet there. You are experiencing *evolution*.

We tend to see many products as revolutionary. Examples include airplanes, personal computers, and communication networks. For the average consumer, it probably seemed one day as if these products were suddenly everywhere. Their advent seemed revolutionary. However, from a technological point of view, the process was far from revolutionary. These products were the result of hundreds of years of evolving technology. The revolution was not the product. Rather, it was the product's impact on the market once the technology became sufficiently mature.

The time from when technology is first proven until there is widespread adoption is often much greater than the originators envision. Broad-based knowledge of how to use a technology most effectively almost always takes much longer than anticipated. It is typical for visionaries to think that they can short-circuit this evolutionary process but they are rarely successful. The market often says, "Not yet."

In such situations, a relationship with the marketplace begins to emerge. Often one or two sales are made, perhaps of custom-built products or systems. In many cases, technical services are sold because there is not yet a product. Few people believe that the path to eventual product success is a long as it probably is.

Evolution situations are central to many of the case histories described in Chapters Five through Seven. Steam-propelled vehicles—boats, trains, and automobiles—were hundreds of years in the offing. Aircraft concepts evolved over many centuries. Flying wings and helicopters took several decades to mature.

In the computer industry, calculators, cash registers, typewriters, and tabulators were far from instant successes. Similarly, it took a long time for word processing, personal computing, spreadsheets, and desktop publishing to become widespread. In fact, computers in general—from mainframes to minis to micros—required many decades to weave themselves into the fabric of our lives.

Examples of evolution situations include the almost fifty years it took Vannevar Bush's vision to evolve into Microsoft's Windows. Another example is the decades that passed between Alan Kay's Dynabook and Apple's PowerBook. Very, very few product concepts go quickly from the visionary's workshop or garage to everybody's office or desktop.

Most visionaries and entrepreneurs feel that they can circumvent evolutionary processes. They point to examples such as Apple, Microsoft, and Sun, which became billion-dollar companies almost overnight. What they fail to see is the tens of thousands of companies whose success came much more slowly if at all. They are also unaware of the earlier years that led up to the success stories. The revolutionary, overnight success is probably a myth or at least a very, very unlikely outcome.

Indications that a company is in an evolution situation include regularly slipped and missed product development and sales targets. Frequent incompatibility problems with existing marketplace infrastructure are also likely. Skepticism in the marketplace and perception of risk rather than of benefits are other indications that the technologies are immature—both the technologies in products and the technologies underlying the processes for development and manufacturing of the products. Such indicators also reflect immaturity of the market or business proposition. That is, the intended compelling reason to buy is often far from compelling. This is especially true for consumers who do not inherently value enabling technologies.

The implications of evolution situations are quite straightforward. Considerable patience with actual progress as opposed to expected progress is needed. Almost continual reselling to top management and investors is required. Other sources of cash flow may be needed as the evolution situation lengthens in time.

For this reason, an evolving new venture may be difficult to sustain while an old venture is waning. Thus, new directions are best started upon when old business ventures are still paying the bills. Of course, this is likely to be a time when people still think that the old businesses will always work.

There tend to be two ways in which evolution situations lead to success. First, if a small enterprise is involved, it usually needs only modest success to continue. Evolution situations, when managed well, often provide a long series of very modest successes that can provide enough cash flow for small operations. In contrast, if a company is large, evolution situations are best played out in parallel with more mature situations. Although these mature situations may be stagnant or in decline, they often can provide cash flow during the evolution of another. The key is to be very clear about how these situations work together.

Crossover

You have sold a few more copies of your travel planning software. But much to your surprise, customers are using it in their offices rather than in their homes. They are using it to plan business trips rather than vacations. You decide that you have to cross over to the business market, shelving your aspirations for the home consumer market. But what about the fifty thousand brochures you have printed, the consumer databases you have bought, the salespeople you have lined up? You hope at least to be able to use the same brochures and salespeople for the new market. Finally, however, you realize that the only things that can successfully cross over are the software and yourself. These are what I call the *few good things* upon which you are going to build your business.

This *crossover* situation occurs when technologies or processes make the transition from one domain to another. A good example is when Henry Ford and Alfred Sloan borrowed manufacturing and business processes from the railroads and other domains and then perfected their application in the automobile industry. Another example is when Raytheon took microwave cooking technology from the military and applied it to the consumer market.

Crossover usually involves just a few good things, not entire enterprises. These good things are used to create substantial competitive advantage in the new domain. The key, of course, is importing or exporting the right things. If you are wrong, there is no advantage. If you hedge and import or export too much then the amount of change may be confusing and perhaps overwhelming. The process of making these choices involves clarifying your relationship with the marketplace. Although this relationship is probably still immature, these choices should be influenced by the type of relationship you are trying to create.

It is no accident that I have used import and export examples to typify crossover. Chapters Five through Seven illustrate both. Ford and Sloan imported. Raytheon exported. Hollerith imported punched-card technology to create the tabulator industry. The British military imported tracked-vehicle technology from the tractor industry to create tanks. Computer technology was originally thought to be primarily of value to science and engineering. However, this technology crossed over to the business machines industry, which eventually provided a much larger market. Thus, crossover situations can work both ways. In either case, however, the key is in choosing the right things that will make a substantial difference.

Search Technology, a software company I head, provides an example of choosing the right things. The division of Search Technology that developed and sold planning and assessment tools matured to the point that an independent company was created. The process of creating this business—Enterprise Support Systems— involved deciding which part of the existing company would cross over to the new company. After careful reflection about how this new business would add value in the marketplace, we determined that much of the existing corporate culture, the cost accounting system, and various aspects of the overall infrastructure were not compatible with the new business. Consequently, we crossed over only three people and a slimmed-down set of business processes, and we outsourced a variety of functions that the older company probably would have attempted to do in-house.

I have experienced similar decision-making processes in such diverse industries as steel, electronics, and software. These companies were careful to avoid burdening the new venture with substantial baggage from the existing business. They also tended to import key technologies and competencies from outside. I have also experienced situations where new ventures sank under the weight of baggage that provided little if any value and demanded substantial attention.

Indicators of the emergence of (or need for) a crossover situation include recognition that necessary or desired market innovations are not possible without additional technologies or processes. Also important to successful crossover is the extent to which a limited number of key technologies or processes are clearly applicable in a targeted domain other than where these technologies or processes originated. Competitive advantage can be gained if the targeted domain is unaware of the potential applicability of these technologies.

A crossover situation can provide substantial competitive advantage if you make the right choices and choose to carry over just the right things. Avoid crossing over technologies and processes from the original domain that are not useful in the new one.

It is important to realize how difficult it can be to cross over just a few good things. People within an existing enterprise usually have great difficulty simply recognizing the baggage associated with such systems as cost accounting and implicit rewards. In addition, there is often strong pressure to bring as much of the old company as possible to the new markets. This often results in the fledgling lifeboat being swamped—and consequently going down with the ship.

Nobody wants to go down with the ship. To avoid this, a plan of how situations will work together should be developed and communicated. The remaining useful life of the ill-fated ship as well as growth rates for the life boats launched should be projected. Understanding what situations the life boats are in—vision quest, evolution, or crossover—is central to developing such a plan.

Crossing the Chasm

By now, you have sold quite a few copies of your software. However, you have sold most of them personally, primarily to people who were intrigued with your travel planning tool and captivated by your enthusiasm. Mail order sales, in contrast, have been disappointing. The few sales you make this way barely cover the costs of advertising and mailings. You decide that you need to change the ways in which you portray the benefits of your software. You have to downplay the gee-whiz technology aspects of it and focus on its practical business value. In the process, you hope you can widen your audience and sell your software to everybody. You are trying to *cross the chasm*.

Geoffrey Moore in *Crossing the Chasm* (1991) discusses the process of moving high-tech products from niche markets to broad markets. The process is cast in terms of a technology adoption life cycle that includes a sequence of customers that he characterizes as *innovators*, *early adopters*, *early majority*, *late majority*, and *laggards*. The chasm occurs between the early selling to innovators and early adopters and the subsequent selling to the rest—in other words, moving beyond friends.

Crossing the chasm is difficult because the reason to buy differs substantially on each side of it. For the innovators and early adopters, the reason to buy often includes the desire to be innovative, to lead paradigm shifts, and to try new approaches in general. In contrast, the early majority and subsequent buyers are more pragmatic and often not particularly technology-oriented.

Moore argues that to cross the chasm and not fall back into it, the enterprise must be transformed. He suggests that crossing over represents a move from being pioneers to becoming settlers. Thus, crossing the chasm requires a change in a company's relationship with the marketplace. Although this relationship is likely to have been narrow and limited, it now must be viewed in broader terms.

Several of my recent experiences in the computer and electronics industries illustrate this situation. These companies had products with performance far superior to the market leaders. They had, up to that point, primarily sold to the portion of the market that was sufficiently sophisticated to appreciate superior performance. Their problems came when they tried to appeal to broader markets. Their natural inclination was to enhance performance further because that was what they knew how to do. But we devoted our attention to other attributes of their offerings—integrating with other technologies, providing supporting services, and lowering prices. Doing these things enabled them to appeal to much larger markets.

The discussion of the transportation industry in Chapter Five provides numerous examples of crossing the chasm situations for railroads, automobiles, and aircraft. Innovators and early adopters quickly invested in these technologies once they were mature. But the mass market was slow to adopt what they perceived to be noisy, smelly, expensive machines.

Similarly, Chapter Six discusses how calculators, cash registers, typewriters, and tabulators were, for the most part, still oddities in the late 1800s and early 1900s. Eventually, however, the early majority and then the late majority adopted these machines in their work. The pattern was similar for mainframe computers in the 1960s, minicomputers in the 1970s, and microcomputers in the 1980s. Indeed, the personal computer industry is just now making headway with the late majority.

Moore (1991) clearly portrays the difficulties of crossing the chasm from innovators and early adopters to the early majority and the late majority. He maintains that the key to crossing the chasm is to develop a market-centered approach. This approach may be contrasted with the technology- or product-centered approach that sustained a company through vision quest, evolution, and crossover situations. Within a well-defined market segment, you should focus on gaining dominant market share in this segment and making your product the de facto standard.

An indicator that a business is in an existing or emerging crossing the chasm situation is sales dominated by purchases by innovators and early adopters. Another indicator is difficulty in convincing pragmatists of the benefits of the product. The firm also may encounter difficulty packaging the product as part of what Moore calls "whole product" solutions, that is, packaging it to enable pragmatists to buy an off-the-shelf solution rather than an individual product.

When a firm is crossing the chasm it has to shift emphasis from the intriguing invention to the compelling problems it can solve and concrete value that it can provide. Packaging of products and services—indeed, the whole approach to marketing and sales—must become market driven.

In my experience, it is very helpful to adopt this kind of thinking early on. As discussed earlier in this chapter, even the vision quest is best if cast in market-oriented rather than technological terms. Admittedly, this is a very difficult thing to do. Fascination with particular technologies may be all that sustains a company when its sales are modest or nonexistent. Nevertheless, the sooner it focuses on creating a compelling market proposition the better.

Steady Growth

It worked! Your more pragmatic sales strategy resulted in a flood of orders. You are shipping more and more software every day. You are hiring people as fast as you can to keep up with the demand. Your financial projections look wonderful. You are thinking about an initial public offering, perhaps in the next twelve to eighteen months. Life is sweet!

The *steady growth* situation emerges after the chasm is crossed. It involves substantial change. This situation is typified by accelerating sales and—one hopes—profits, as well as more people and greater specialization. Market share may be increasing. When technology-based products are involved, the market size may also continue to grow. Increasing volumes are shipped. Primary difficulties are tactical and operational problems associated with meeting demand.

The nature of the relationship with the marketplace at this time may be likened to romance. Most enterprises want to experience it. Yet this situation sets the stage for situations to come because most if not all key people become trapped by their tasks at this time. Consequently, strategic tasks are given less and less attention. Everyone is so busy fighting forest fires that no one is planting trees.

I have experienced this situation—or rather its aftermath—with a variety of companies. During the Reagan years, many large and small defense companies grew dramatically. Several companies that I work with went public during that period, as well as more recently, and doubled (or more than doubled) their sales for two or three years in a row.

Those heady times led to their hiring many more employees and to rapidly growing infrastructures. People behaved as if such dramatic growth rates could continue forever. But for defense, at least, the party ended. Steady growth faded and new situations, like those described in the following sections, emerged. As surprising as it may sound, executives in defense companies told me they were taken unawares. They had not expected the boom to end and were not prepared for it.

The implications are clear: steady growth is great but you can't relax for long. Few companies are able to stay in the steady growth situation. They need to anticipate transitions to other situations. Thoughtful situation assessment and planning can enable changing the nature, and perhaps the types, of transitions that a company will experience. In some cases, transitions through other situations can be expedited and the company put back into steady growth. (I discuss the nature of these transitions in Chapter Three.)

A *Business Week* cover story (Zellner and others, 1995) provided strong evidence that companies are able to experience more frequent steady growth situations by intentionally dealing with the possibilities of transitions to less desirable situations. The article profiled ten companies, including technology leaders Hewlett Packard, Motorola, Intel, and Microsoft. Among the many lessons learned by these leading companies, the first was, "Accept change."

In the context of this book, that lesson means that businesses must understand potential transitions and approach them creatively in order to deal with them earlier and better than their competitors.

Consolidation

After many months of shipping truckload after truckload of software packages, you begin to feel that steady growth will last forever. Unfortunately, it does not. Almost overnight, it seems, lots of companies are selling travel planning software. In fact, too many are doing so. All are trying to take market share away from your company. You have no choice but to cut prices. Everyone is cutting prices. Your margins are steadily shrinking. A few of your competitors are merging and the competition is getting even stiffer. You decide to acquire some other players. You are in the middle of *consolidation*.

Consolidation situations often start when technologies become sufficiently mature to achieve market entry. As discussed earlier, this maturity involves not just the product technology but also the technology necessary for manufacturing, support, marketing, and sales. The initial market success attracts, often quickly, a dramatic increase in the number of players. Each of these players scrambles for market share, which may be relatively easy during the market's initial growth stages. But eventually market share only comes with lower prices and often higher costs, for example, for increased expenditures for marketing and sales.

As a result, there are lower gross and net profit margins. There is a substantial reduction in discretionary funds. However, in order to remain in the game, there usually is an increased need for capital. This leads, almost inevitably, to firms leaving the market, merging, being acquired, and consolidating in general.

Consolidation situations often reflect missed opportunities because of outright product failures. In other cases, consolidation situations occur when companies are unable to transform themselves from one technology paradigm to another. Companies may also find themselves in consolidation situations if they fail to focus on the areas where the competition is heading. For example, Remington-Rand was unable to focus on the computer business. In contrast, International Business Machines (IBM) did.

I have frequently seen the consolidation situation among the defense contractors I work with. As everyone knows, the competition for declining defense budgets is intense. Price has become predominant in all but a few specialized areas. Trying to stay afloat, companies compromise profit objectives and sometimes even sell below cost to avoid idling resources.

Computer manufacturers have also commonly experienced the consolidation situation over the past few years. With personal computers now selling better than television sets, most personal computer manufacturers have clearly crossed the chasm. Several have experienced a period of steady growth. Now, however, margins have dropped substantially as numerous new clones on the market keep prices low. By keeping their costs of sales low—using third-party and mail-order channels—these competitors still manage to be reasonably profitable.

Chapter Five describes many consolidation situations. Hundreds or thousands of companies blossomed in the steamboat, railroad, automobile, and aircraft industries. But after consolidation only a few of them remained. The forerunners of the computer industry—namely, manufacturers of calculators, cash registers, typewriters, and tabulators—experienced the same consequences, as illustrated in Chapter Six. The adoption of what I call the Pac-man strategy in the defense industry, discussed in Chapter Seven, has resulted in significant consolidation. Lockheed acquired General Dynamics' aircraft division. Martin-Marietta acquired General Electric's military electronics division. Northrop acquired Grumman. Raytheon acquired E Systems. Most recently, Lockheed and Martin merged. Numerous small defense contractors have merged or left the market. Given the state of the defense industry, more consolidation is very likely.

Indicators that a company is in an emerging consolidation situation are obvious. An increasing number of players are scrambling for market share. There are pressures to decrease prices while marketing and sales costs are increasing. Eroding gross and net margins are typical, resulting in decreased discretionary resources. There is a capital crunch at the same time that more funds are needed to compete.

The implications for most companies are also quite clear. At some point, the number of players will start to decrease dramatically as many companies go out of business or are acquired. The choice is either cash in to gain capital for other ventures or be prepared to spend capital to acquire market share. Companies who remain in the competition can do quite well, although substantial long-term debt may be incurred.

There are several strategies for avoiding or short-circuiting consolidation situations. One strategy is to spin off or sell mature businesses. Another is to milk the cash cow that such businesses represent but avoid investments. A compelling strategy is to make one's own mature products obsolete by frequently introducing new products. If a company is fast enough, its new products may preempt maturation of its old ones and, thereby, prevent the emergence of conditions conducive to consolidation. Hewlett Packard, for example, pursues this strategy.

Silent War

Your sales manager brings you a brochure that he picked up on an overseas sales trip. Your biggest competitor in terms of number of copies of software sold is now a company that you never believed could make it in the travel planning market. You knew it had been trying to do so for the past few years but you did not expect it to succeed. Your sales manager tells you that this competitor will soon be releasing tools that are more advanced than yours are. They offer better graphics and animation and an embedded expert travel adviser. In addition, they will be sold at prices much lower than yours. This unexpected event means that you are caught in a *silent war*.

The victors who emerge from a consolidation situation may be able to relax briefly. However, new challenges are likely to arise.

One of these challenges is discussed by Ira Magaziner and Mark Patinkin in their book, *The Silent War* (1989). The set of circumstances surrounding silent war situations involves one or more of several scenarios. A successful enterprise, perhaps a victor of consolidation, does not realize that competitors are emerging. Alternatively, it may realize this but discount it. Or an enterprise either does not realize that new technologies are maturing or does realize it but discounts these technologies. In all of these cases, the company is in a competitive war without realizing it. Consequently, while the company assumes that its relationship with the marketplace is a steady one, it may be seriously threatened.

As noted earlier, often this enterprise is busy fighting forest fires and perhaps reengineering to get better and better at fighting fires. It doesn't notice the other aggressive foresters or even the new types of trees that have cropped up, in some cases fire-resistant trees. When the competition emerges suddenly it may be too late to respond effectively.

My business went through this situation a few years ago. Without thinking much about it I had assumed that most, if not all, advanced R&D on intelligent decision support systems occurred in the United States, Japan, and Europe. Consequently, in this aspect of the business we paid attention only to developments in these regions, with an obvious bias toward the United States.

My awakening came when I was invited to speak at meetings. I found substantial representation there from developing nations. Much to my surprise, I learned that there are R&D centers in some of these countries that specialize in areas in which I did not think they could possibly be players. Talking with some of the people from these centers, I heard many novel and interesting ideas. I also discovered that my company had unexpected competitors. I was told that the intelligent software market is easy to enter because of low capital costs. Only a few smart people, often educated abroad, are needed. Companies can bootstrap from there.

The implication for my business, and for many others, is that raw technical talent is not unique and is becoming less so. I began to realize that the competitive advantage of my company's software lies in its content rather than the mere fact of its creation. The context-specific intelligence built into our software provides more advantage than the hardware and software technologies that enable creation of these products simply because many other companies have expertise in these same enabling technologies.

Chapters Five through Seven discuss numerous instances of silent war situations. The impact of the railroads on the stage-coaches and canal boats, of the automobile on the railroads, and of Japanese process improvements on U.S. automakers provide excellent illustrations of such situations. Other examples in the transportation industry are the impact on U.S. aircraft manufacturers of the development of the jet engine by the British and Germans and the innovations of the Airbus consortium.

Silent war situations also occurred in the computer industry. The emergence of electronic computing in the 1940s is one example. The development of minicomputers and, subsequently, personal computers constituted silent wars relative to previous computer systems. The emergence of software as the high-margin segment of the industry—while the profitability of hardware plummeted—is yet another example.

Again, the wars were silent because the dominant players either did not pay attention to or noticed but dismissed the potential competition. When these wars became increasingly audible, people were caught off guard and often responded less than adequately. The primary reason these responses were inadequate was lack of attention rather than the nature of the competition.

Indicators that a company is in a silent war situation include potential new players nipping at the heels of the major players. When nonmainstream solutions to customers' problems within your market segments increase, they too indicate potential new players. Also indicative are relevant new technologies appearing in the technical literature, usually first in science publications and subsequently in engineering publications. The maturation of new technologies in other domains may indicate potential migration of these technologies to your market segments.

A company in a silent war situation needs to recognize it as early as possible. This may be accomplished by forming its own new ventures to nibble at its own heels—in other words, to be its own toughest competitor. Such companies also need to aggressively pursue new technologies through R&D, consortia, alliances, or acquisitions to assure continued competitive advantage.

Perhaps the best way to deal with silent war situations is to assume that you are always in one. Inevitably new technologies are being created that will compete with yours, even if the developers of these technologies do not realize it. One of them will eventually realize it. With your inside knowledge of your own products and plans, you can be the first with this recognition. This depends, however, on avoiding being trapped looking inward. You need to delegate forest fire fighting and spend your time investigating new types of trees, planting some of them, and ensuring that they are sheltered from the heat of the daily fires.

Paradigm Lost

Your marketing and engineering managers bring you an article from an industry magazine. In it you learn that one of your strongest competitors has perfected a process that enables selling travel planning software, including daily updates of key databases, over computer networks such as the Internet rather than at retail stores and through mail order. The result is no packaging, no inventory, minimal sales force, and so on. This reduces that company's cost of sales to one-tenth of yours. Your engineers have been working on a network-based process, using somewhat different technology, but it is not fully developed yet. Furthermore, they are projecting only 50 percent cost reductions with it. Your marketing and distribution paradigm is lost. You realize that soon you may no longer be a player.

I borrowed the name of this situation from John Casti's wonderful book, *Paradigms Lost* (1989). The book deals with the passing of scientific paradigms. My interest is in technology and business paradigms. I define the term *paradigm* in the sense that Joel Arthur Barker used in his book, *Paradigms* (1993). That is, a business paradigm is a set of values, priorities, and practices that define the boundaries of business activities. In addition, a business paradigm provides guidance, often implicitly, for how to behave within these boundaries in order to be successful.

A paradigm lost situation emerges when a new technology or business practice displaces an old technology or practice. Quite often, those who perfected the old technologies or practices are reluctant to accept this change. They are left standing in the starting gate while the race begins. They simply cannot believe that the old way is not still the best. The result can be that they are no longer a player and their relationship with the marketplace dissolves.

Adopting the new paradigm may require new management or at least a succession, such as from Thomas J. Watson Sr. to Thomas J. Watson Jr. It also involves playing catch-up, probably a new experience for those who designed the old paradigm. Obviously, the sooner a company realizes that the paradigm has changed or is likely to change the better.

I work with many enterprises that have experienced this situation. In the steel industry, the large integrated steel producers were surprised by the highly efficient minimills that use nonunion labor, continuous casters, and other innovations. In the software industry, the mainframe software providers, who had modeled themselves on IBM, found that both the mainframe and their models were no longer the dominant paradigms. Numerous defense contractors found that the post–World War II business model began to disappear when the Berlin Wall fell and the Soviet Union broke apart. In all three of these examples, the companies only recognized these paradigm changes after the marketplace had been sending strong signals for many years.

I have experienced a more subtle example of this situation with companies involved with environmental regulations because of their products or their manufacturing processes. Many have developed substantial expertise in arguing against tougher regulations as well as in defending the relatively benign nature of their products and processes. However, in the past few years, a fundamental change—a new paradigm—has emerged. Several companies are now viewing increased environmental regulation as an economic opportunity. They have realized, for example, that abilities for toxic-free manufacturing and demanufacturing for recycling may be substantial competitive advantages. As they have attempted to improve these abilities in their companies, they have often encountered substantial resistance from colleagues trapped in the old paradigm.

Meeting resistance is common. A few people in a company realize that the market paradigm has changed or is about to change. In some cases, as in the defense industry, the evidence may be overwhelming. Still, internal forces will not accept it. They discount and dismiss it. Consequently, those who wish to change paradigms often face long, uphill battles.

Paradigm lost situations are found throughout the case histories described in Chapters Five through Seven. In the automobile industry, European craft producers were slow to adopt mass production while U.S. mass producers were slow to adopt lean production. In the aircraft industry, Douglas Aircraft Company hesitated in shifting from piston engines to jet engines. All the aircraft and avionics companies with which I work have been struck by the implications of viewing the aircraft as a computer cabinet rather than as the primary value in itself.

There have been many examples in the computer industry too. Watson, Sr. had great difficulty adapting from punched cards to magnetic tape. IBM discounted the emergence of minicomputers. Both IBM and Digital Equipment Corporation (DEC) discounted the potential of computer workstations and personal computers. Olsen at DEC was reluctant to embrace time-sharing, build 16-bit machines, and outsource elements of computer manufacturing. And all the computer companies with which I work have yet to internalize fully the concept that software is the high-margin element of the computer market.

The defense industry—including companies, government, and universities—continue to have difficulty letting go of the Cold War paradigm. I have encountered defense executives who claim that their companies were caught unawares despite the headlines of the past eight to ten years that heralded this industry's decline. This shows their depth of attachment to the old paradigm. Traditional beliefs about R&D, technology, performance, costs, and so on are becoming outmoded in many ways, but this industry is having tremendous difficulty adopting market-oriented beliefs.

In all of these examples, the old paradigm started to become dysfunctional long before the market leaders recognized it. They continued to get better and better within the context of the old paradigm. They were not entertaining new paradigms because doing so would be inconsistent with their dedication to optimizing their abilities within the reigning paradigm.

Ironically, this tendency is probably good for the economy as a whole. As long as we needed buggy whips, it was useful that one or more companies tried to produce the best buggy whips possible. Once buggy whips were no longer needed, these companies' investments in this paradigm became obsolete. Although this was not a problem for consumers, it was a major problem for those who had invested themselves totally in the buggy whip paradigm.

Several indicators can help identify when paradigm lost situations are emerging. Are the dominant technologies or processes underlying your products and services becoming less central in other domains? Are your technologies or processes unable to meet market expectations for performance, quality, and cost? Are new and growing players emerging in your markets who do not employ improved versions of your technologies or processes?

Paradigm lost situations have important implications. There are the obvious and substantial risks of ceasing to be a major player or a player at all. Once this situation is evident it is too late to catch up through R&D. Alliances or acquisitions are likely to be necessary to change paradigms quickly. Of course, a company can always withdraw from the market segments affected by the change.

The chances of successfully avoiding this situation or at least transitioning through it quickly depends on adopting a critical assumption. That is, every company must assume that there are paradigm lost situations waiting in the future. The only uncertainty is the timing and, of course, the nature of the new paradigm.

Once a company adopts this assumption, it needs to focus on when to abandon the current paradigm. It wants to do this before the paradigm is lost but not while it still dominates the marketplace. The safest way to be neither too early or too late is to maintain the old paradigm while also investing in, or at least monitoring, new paradigms. The old paradigm may be central to mature situations while the new one plays a role in emerging situations such as vision quest, evolution, and crossover situations.

Commodity Trap

Travel planning software is now a standard element on everybody's computer. Almost all businesses, large and small, use it. Millions of copies, primarily updates, are sold every year. You are one of a handful of companies remaining in this market. The planning tools have also become very similar; differentiation has disappeared. All that matters now is price, quality, and service. You are constantly looking for ways to cut prices while also improving quality and service. All of your competitors are trying to do the same. You are stuck in a *commodity trap*.

Eventually, any really good idea becomes ubiquitous. Everybody wants it. Everybody understands what it has to be. Unfortunately, everybody can also produce it. The competitive situation at this point involves selling basically the same thing that all competitors are selling. The emphasis is on producing and selling quality products at low cost. Sales volumes and market share are what count. Each company's relationship with the marketplace is that of just another vendor.

This is a difficult situation for companies who are used to selling unique functionality. For example, in the past a sales force may have been expensive but very good at explaining the product and how to use it. Now, no one needs or is willing to pay for this level of support.

We are all aware of a variety of commodities on the market: food, clothing, and basic materials such as steel are a few examples. Cars have become commodities too. Most cars look alike because all car designers deal with the same principles of aerodynamics. This is also true, of course, for airplane designers.

Consumer electronics products and computers today also quickly become commodities. The company that introduces a new microprocessor usually has a very brief period of substantial competitive advantage—perhaps a few months—before lower-priced clones become available. Software clones are also becoming widespread.

The companies that I work with in these industries have often been slow to recognize that they are in commodity trap situations. In my experience, it is very difficult to accept that what one has long viewed as high-tech innovation—for example, subsonic aircraft— are now commodities. Aircraft company executives have only recently acknowledged this situation.

If you find yourself in this situation, there are two ways to transition to a new situation. The predominant method is to move into a process situation, as described in the next section. The second alternative is to pursue vision quest, evolution, or crossover situations in order to pull your market offerings out of the commodity category. For example, as an automobile or aircraft manufacturer, you might focus on providing more value—unique value, one hopes. Perhaps you will offer driver or pilot information systems or passenger entertainment systems. In fact, this is what these industries are focusing on today.

The indicators of a commodity trap situation are straightforward. Everybody is selling basically the same thing. Quality, service, and especially price are all that matters. There are high costs of marketing and sales as each company tries to differentiate its product or service from the rest. Deep discounts are often necessary because of the price sensitivity of commodity markets. Increased costs and decreased prices lead to low gross and net margins.

Commodity trap situations can be a terrible experience and usually are. However, transition to a steady growth situation is possible, especially if the process situation is quickly pursued.

There is also the possibility of revisiting the consolidation situation as the number of players continues to shrink. To succeed one must be one of the survivors. Unlike transitions from steady growth to consolidation, where a company may be able to cash in by selling its market share, transitions from commodity trap to consolidation seldom provide such valuable consolation prizes. Instead, market share is simply taken from the losers who then may sell their remaining assets at fire-sale prices. Transitions to a process situation and success in it may be the only way to avoid this fate.

Process Situations

For your software company to survive and squeeze out profits that are acceptable to financial analysts and pension funds, you have to focus on your processes. Your sole goal is to produce planning tools that are better rather than different. You apply quality management everywhere possible. You reengineer every process you can identify. You have fewer and fewer people trying to do more and more by— you hope—working smarter rather than harder. You have become a star player in a *process situation*.

A company is in a process situation when it realizes that success in its markets depends more on process innovations that on product innovations. The emphasis shifts to manufacturing, marketing and sales, and other processes rather than new product development. Process improvements become the keys to increased quality, decreased time to market, and profits. The goal is to be better rather than different.

Although doing this sounds simple, it may not fit easily into a culture where product innovations have always been thought of as key to success. It may not fit into a culture that has yet to accept that the computer or airplane it offers is now a commodity. It may be very difficult for a company to accept that its relationship with the marketplace has evolved into one of many vendors, even if it is among the best.

Thus, the process situation may be relevant but not recognized. The competitors who quickly recognize the need to pursue this situation are likely to be the ones who continue to succeed. Indeed, in some cases the most successful process innovators were not even on the scene when product innovations were central.

The automobile industry probably offers the best example of this situation. Lean manufacturing, with its focus on decreasing costs, increasing quality, and decreasing time to market, emerged in Japan, has penetrated much of the United States, and has started to infiltrate Europe.

Business process reengineering has become a central philosophy for companies in this situation. Cost cutting through delayering, downsizing, rightsizing, outsourcing, and so on are being emphasized in most industries. The goal is to be the lowest-cost, highest-quality vendor among the many in the marketplace.

In my experience, innovative companies are not content with process situations. Although they may focus on being very good at this situation within their traditional product lines, they also invest substantial energy in exploring new products and new approaches. These explorations usually result in a new situation emerging—for instance, a vision quest situation—that is played out in parallel with their mainstream process situation.

For example, a mid-sized company with which I am currently working provides a range of products and services in the telecommunications market. In our discussions, the CEO has concluded that all of these offerings will be obsolete within five years. Therefore, he is deeply involved in a process situation to maximize the return on his investments in these offerings. But at the same time, we are pursuing a new situation, probably a crossover situation, that will sustain the company's growth as the current products and services fade.

Thus, the process situation need not be the end of the line. It may signal maturation and decline for a particular set of market offerings. However, if what is happening is understood, especially if it is seen coming, it is possible to explore and invest in new situations long before the end of a particular situation results in the end of the enterprise.

Process situations are common in the case histories. Chapter Five discusses how Ford and Sloan both pursued process innovations in terms of mass production and professional management, respectively. Japanese lean production innovations reflect a process situation. More recently, Ford has been involved in a process situation focused on lean production. In my work with the Rover Group, I have found that it too is pursuing an innovative version of the process situation.

Chapter Six explains how IBM, DEC, and Apple have all come to focus on the costs of goods sold and the costs of selling. They realize that their processes have to be streamlined and probably redesigned to achieve acceptable margins. For example, they have all shifted the emphasis to third-party sales channels rather than rely exclusively on their own direct sales force. If they do not pursue such changes, companies with many fewer infrastructure burdens will continually gain market share.

Chapter Seven talks about how defense companies must deal with significant process problems if they are to succeed in nondefense markets. Their processes for marketing and sales are far too rudimentary to provide a basis for success, while their costs of providing the goods that they sell are inflated. Defense conversion usually requires fundamental rather than incremental process improvements.

How does a company know that it's involved in a process situation? One indicator is the extent to which product innovations are of less value because de facto or actual industry standards have emerged. Another is increased pressures to decrease costs of goods sold as well as costs of sales as a percentage of sales. Emphasis on process improvements also increases when financial ratios such as gross and net margins are worse than industry averages. These types of comparisons are particularly relevant when everybody is selling the same thing.

In a process situation, the company recognizes that competitive advantages can be gained only through process improvements. Thus, a shift from a product to a process orientation must be made. There is a substantial risk in this situation. Involvement in process reengineering and continuous quality improvement can completely displace consideration of new products and new situations. Cost cutting through delayering, downsizing, rightsizing, outsourcing, and so on may be necessary and helpful but these activities are unlikely to be sufficient for long-term success. Being the quickest, highest-quality, and lowest-cost producer of an obsolete product is hardly a victory. Thus, the short-term rewards of transitioning from process to steady growth situations through cost cutting should be invested in the creation of new long-term situations.

Summary

The discussion in this chapter provides an important basis for the situation assessment methodology. What do the ten common situations discussed in this chapter have to say about the ability of enterprises to anticipate, recognize, and respond to change in their relationships with their markets? Anticipating such changes means expecting that they can happen. Recognizing these changes means monitoring cues—leading indicators are best—that are predictive of the onset of changes. Responding means deciding that internal changes are necessary or desired and committing to a plan to make these changes.

Enterprises are much better at responding than at anticipating and recognizing. But if everyone admits that changes must be made when there are still sufficient resources remaining, then a reasonable response is possible. Unfortunately, many enterprises accept the need for change only after they have invested most of their discretionary resources in trying to avoid change and maintain the status quo.

The underlying constant is that enterprises do not expect changes in relationships with their markets. They expect the future to be just like the past, perhaps a bit better. They look only for cues that support these expectations. As a result, it takes a crisis to get their attention. But by the time a crisis occurs, it may be too late to respond effectively.

So what should they do? On one level the answer is obvious: pay attention. On a deeper level, however, the answer involves understanding the likely transitions between situations and anticipating these situations and their implications.

Although most enterprises would like permanently to experience a steady growth situation, it is very, very unlikely that they will. However, it is more likely to happen for those who realize how unlikely it is. If you realize that consolidation, silent war, and paradigm lost situations are always just around the corner, you are much more likely to plan creatively. You are more likely to pursue new vision quest, evolution, and crossover situations long before they seem to be needed but while they are in fact still possible.

3

Recognizing Where You Are Headed

The Five Most Common Business Stories—and How Companies Respond

The ten common situations that were described in Chapter Two and the case studies that will be discussed in the chapters to come suggest several predominant transitions between these situations. Figure 3.1 provides a graphic representation of these common transitions. Anticipating, recognizing, and responding to these transitions are important elements of strategic thinking and should strongly influence strategic planning.

The pattern of transitions between situations that each company experiences constitutes its story. This chapter tells several common stories. It also considers the ways in which companies are likely to pursue their stories. The second half of this chapter is devoted to a discussion of how the desirable can be achieved and the undesirable avoided. It concludes with consideration of correlates of successful change.

How Business Patterns Create Stories

During their lifetimes companies are involved in many of the ten common situations and experience the transitions between them. *Stories* are the result.

FIGURE 3.1. Transitions Between the Ten Common Situations.

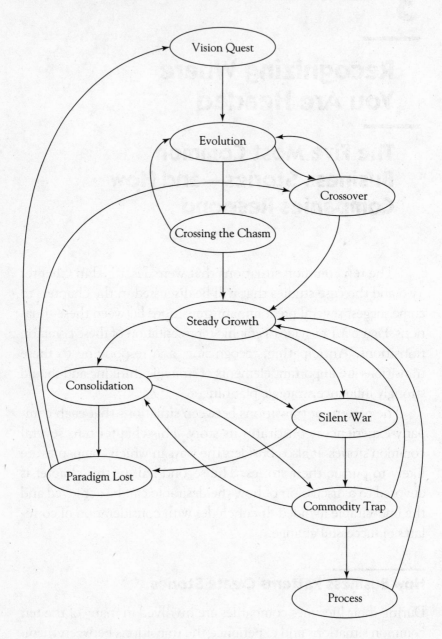

There are five common stories. I call them *classic life cycle, false start, death spiral, reinventing the company,* and *branching and pruning.* These stories encompass both desirable and undesirable patterns of business situations.

Classic Life Cycle

The classic life cycle story is told in many management books. It typically involves birth, growth, maturation, and decline. Put in the terms of the ten common situations, the story created is as follows:

VISION QUEST–EVOLUTION–CROSSOVER–
CROSSING THE CHASM–STEADY GROWTH–
CONSOLIDATION–SILENT WAR–PARADIGM
LOST–COMMODITY TRAP–PROCESS

You may recognize this as the story of the software company and its travel planning products presented in Chapter Two. This story can also be seen to reflect the broader patterns of situations that are described in Chapter One. That is, the first four situations—vision quest, evolution, crossover, and crossing the chasm—occur when a company is ahead of the market. Crossing the chasm can occur again when the marketing is catching up, as can steady growth and consolidation. Finally, silent war, paradigm lost, and possibly commodity trap and process situations occur when the market begins to pass the company by. Thus, the ten common situations provide finer detail within the broad patterns.

This business life cycle is often depicted as inevitable. However, this is not true. The cover story in the February 1995 issue of *Business Week* (Zellner and others, 1995) provides evidence to the contrary by describing companies that have managed to avoid the downside of the cycle. A more comprehensive and compelling view of such companies is provided by James C. Collins and Jerry I. Porras in *Built to Last* (1994), which explains how companies such as Hewlett Packard and Motorola continue to renew themselves.

You too may avoid playing out the classic story. There is no reason why you must experience all of the ten common situations. At the very least, you should not have to remain in these situations for long.

The key to avoiding playing out the classic story is to focus on the ten common situations rather than on the story as a whole. It is too difficult to avoid the story as a whole because the problem becomes too complex and abstract. Instead, you need to focus on bite-size chunks of the stories, that is, on situations.

An analogy may serve to illustrate this concept. If a person focuses on becoming slim, the task may seem overwhelming. However, if a person focuses on avoiding snacks after dinner, he or she will eventually become slimmer. The key is defining manageable problems whose solutions contribute to resolution of the problem as a whole.

False Start

The false start is a common story among new ventures. It also is common for new product lines within existing companies. There are two versions of this story; both are stories of continually trying to gain momentum and then losing it:

VISION QUEST–EVOLUTION–
CROSSOVER–EVOLUTION

OR

VISION QUEST–EVOLUTION-CROSSING THE
CHASM–EVOLUTION

I have encountered this story frequently among university spin-offs. These new ventures are formed on the basis of one technical idea. In the United States, the company may be seeded through a Small Business Innovation Research (SBIR) contract with the federal government. In principle, this seed money and perhaps a second round of such funding will result in commercialization of the founding technical idea. However, what frequently happens is that these ventures repeatedly apply for SBIR contracts. I have known a couple of companies who have won over a hundred such contracts without ever getting a product to market. People who manage small business incubators, which are prevalent at U.S. universities, have told me of many companies that settle in to focus solely on SBIR contracts. I have seen the same behaviors in small companies supported by similar mechanisms in other countries.

I have also experienced this story in much larger companies that attempt to launch new product lines that are different from their existing product lines. A good recent example in the United States is the many companies who have entertained pursuing the health care market. I have worked with four defense electronics companies who considered applying their technologies and skills to either medical electronics or health information systems. One company actually made a large sale but the customer then went bankrupt. Two other companies have transitioned from evolution to crossover to evolution at least once. The fourth company developed a business plan quickly, evaluated its chances of success, and decided to terminate the effort. This last is the only success story among the four.

You may wonder why I call it a success story. This company quickly developed and evaluated an alternative but then stopped all investment in the alternative when it determined that it was not the best choice. That is good planning. Considering an alternative does not mean that it must be pursued. In fact, if a company is only willing to consider alternatives that it is sure it will subsequently pursue, it is being much too conservative. A key to avoiding undesirable situations is the ability—and willingness—to consider and evaluate quickly a variety of ways of proceeding.

Death Spiral

Companies want to avoid false starts. If they get into them, they want to exit them quickly. They also want to avoid death spirals or, again, to find their way out of them quickly. The death spiral story is probably quite familiar too:

STEADY GROWTH–CONSOLIDATION–
COMMODITY TRAP–CONSOLIDATION

It should be noted that in this and the following stories the way in which steady growth was initially achieved is not central and thus I do not discuss it.

As told in Chapter Five, 2,500 railroad companies in 1850 were reduced to 30 in 1900. Comparable stories unfolded for the steamboat, automobile, and aircraft industries. Chapter Six discusses similar stories for the calculator, cash register, typewriter, and tabulator industries. Today, many companies or business units within companies are caught in death spirals. The best recent example is that of the defense industry, as discussed more fully in Chapter Seven. In the past few years Lockheed acquired the aircraft division of General Dynamics, Martin-Marietta acquired the military electronics division of General Electric (GE), Northrop acquired Grumman, Raytheon acquired E Systems, and Lockheed and Martin merged. In addition, numerous small defense contractors merged or left the market.

If you live through this story, you want to be among the companies that survive or are acquired under attractive terms. Simply closing your doors and selling your hard assets is not a desirable outcome, although many companies, especially lower-tiered subcontractors—that is, subcontractors of subcontractors—have little other choice.

For would-be acquirers with the available resources, the prevalence of death spiral stories can be a wonderful thing. I have worked with companies who made acquisitions for no cash and the assumption of the acquired company's debt, which was promptly renegotiated with the financial institutions involved. In one case, the acquirer made back its investment in six months.

If you do not have the resources—or the energy—to acquire other players, then make yourself as attractive as possible. That is, maximize short-term sales and profits, avoid investments, and make your financial statements look as rosy as possible. You can also try to break out of the death spiral by redeploying your resources in other markets where there are fewer players or less capable players. The following two stories are examples of how this might be accomplished.

Reinventing the Company

One way of avoiding classic life cycles and death spirals is to reinvent a company or, in effect, to create a new company. There are two common versions of this story:

STEADY GROWTH–CONSOLIDATION–
PARADIGM LOST–CROSSOVER–
STEADY GROWTH

OR

STEADY GROWTH–CONSOLIDATION–
PARADIGM LOST–VISION QUEST–EVOLUTION–
CROSSING THE CHASM–STEADY GROWTH

These two versions of the story involve either encountering a paradigm lost situation or precipitating one. In the former case, a company has little choice but to react. In the latter, it may choose to act much earlier than necessary but while it still has the resources to do so.

In the first version of the story, a company makes a transition to a crossover situation by either acquiring technology and people or moving its own technology and people to new markets. In the second pattern, a company creates the technology and grows internally the people needed for competitive advantage. If management is skilled at accomplishing these transitions, it may be able to keep the company continually growing by harvesting resources from declining stories and reinvesting these resources in potential growth stories.

The best example of a company that is highly skilled in this manner is Motorola. I have had the good fortune to work with three Motorola business units and about two hundred managers and executives. Motorola started in batteries, moved to radios and televisions, and then moved again to semiconductors, pagers, cellular phones, and other products. This process continues today, with the latest vision quest being the satellite communications network Iridium.

A particularly important aspect of the way in which Motorola and others reinvent themselves involves entertaining and investing in multiple stories. Some of these stories turn out to be false starts and investment in them is stopped. Some become modest successes and may or may not be continued. A few—and only a few are needed—become significant successes. These receive substantial investment until paradigm lost situations emerge or are precipitated.

Branching and Pruning

The branching and pruning story is another way to avoid the classic life cycle and death spiral. Three common versions of this story are as follows:

> STEADY GROWTH–CONSOLIDATION–
> PARADIGM LOST–COMMODITY TRAP–
> PROCESS–STEADY GROWTH
>
> OR
>
> STEADY GROWTH–CONSOLIDATION–
> PARADIGM LOST–CROSSOVER–STEADY GROWTH
>
> OR
>
> STEADY GROWTH–CONSOLIDATION–
> PARADIGM LOST–VISION QUEST–EVOLUTION–
> CROSSING THE CHASM–STEADY GROWTH

This story resembles that of reinventing the company, with a few important exceptions. First, these companies do not necessarily make the transition away from mature markets. Second, they actively encourage the pursuit of a large number of versions of these stories—in other words, there is much branching. Third, they communicate very clear criteria for continued investment in a story, that is, there is decisive pruning.

Collins and Porras's *Built to Last* (1994), from which I borrowed the name of this story, provides a detailed discussion of an exemplary brancher and pruner, namely, Minnesota Mining and Manufacturing Company (3M). The company, which is well known for its many divisions and hundreds of product lines, is constantly branching and pruning.

In my interactions with 3M, I have been impressed with the autonomy of its divisions. All clearly understand the branching and pruning process, which they usually have replicated locally. This company's continued success provides substantial evidence of the power that comes when a company understands its relationships with its markets, probable changes in them, and ways to respond quickly and remain innovative in them.

A Review

In this section of this chapter I have described five typical business stories and shown how they are made up of the ten common situations. These stories also illustrate how particular patterns of situations lead to specific consequences for the companies that play them out. However, as emphasized earlier, companies should not focus on pursuing or avoiding these stories as a whole. Instead, they should focus on the situations and transitions between situations. Once again, the focus on where they are will help them get where they want to go.

The ten common situations and five common stories provide a reasonably comprehensive picture of *what* happens to companies. The obvious next question concerns *how* it happens. Answering this question requires an exploration of how companies respond to change—how they pursue their stories.

How Stories Are Pursued

It all seems very simple. Situation assessment and strategic thinking are straightforward processes. Companies should pursue desirable situations and avoid undesirable situations or, at the very least, make the transition from undesirable to desirable situations as quickly as possible. If they do this, they create a successful business story.

Thus, this is what you need to do. However, the key issue remains how to do it. How should you pursue and avoid situations? How should you make transitions happen quickly? The principle is simple, but the practice is much more complicated.

I'll start with descriptive, rather than prescriptive, answers to these questions. How do companies deal with the situations that they encounter or anticipate encountering? How do companies accomplish transitions?

The answer depends on the "mental models" that companies have of themselves and their relationships with their markets. Their abilities to assess their strategic situations are highly influenced by the ways in which they envision using the resulting assessments. Both the current and future situations considered will depend on their mental models of the degree of freedom they have to respond to change. I have found repeatedly that the mental models of executives and managers tend to constrain greatly their consideration of the future. Thus, it is very important to understand the underlying models that determine the perspective with which a company will address strategic issues.

In *Images of Organization* (1986), Gareth Morgan describes several mental models:

1. *The machine model* focuses on the structural aspects of an organization and deals with change by decomposing and recomposing the enterprise.

2. *The organism model* emphasizes the role of the enterprise in its environment, including issues of organizational species and evolution.

3. *The brain model* deals with communication between organizational nodes and learning through feedback.

4. *The cultural model* focuses on the effects of beliefs, routines, and rituals on organizational behaviors.

5. *The political model* emphasizes interests, conflicts, and power and their effects on organizational problem solving and decision making.

Which of these models best describes your organization? Which best describes how the members of your organization think about things? Clearly, all of these views capture some truths about most companies. However, I have found that the two extreme ways in which companies deal with situations and transitions between situations can be expressed in a relatively simple dichotomy.

Synthetic and Organic Perspectives

One of the two points of view is the *synthetic*. This point of view encompasses Morgan's machine model, parts of the brain model (probably the left side), and elements of the political model. The central premise of this point of view is that you can design—synthesize—a company to pursue your mission, goals, and strategies. When changes are needed, you simply redesign the organizational structure, jobs, tasks, reward systems, and so on.

The other point of view is the *organic*. This perspective encompasses Morgan's organism and cultural models, parts of the brain model (the right side, of course), and much of the political model. The premise of this point of view is that you are but one actor within the social system of your company and its environment. Although you may be one of the lead actors, you cannot fully control what happens and how your company evolves. You have to work within the values, beliefs, and preferences of other people and other companies.

The two perspectives have radically different implications for the ways in which one can anticipate, recognize, and respond to current and emerging situations. The synthetic perspective focuses on the ability to design and redesign the company. When the company senses deviations from desired states (for example, sales and profits) it compensates by reorganizing. When this point of view is adopted, the company delayers, downsizes, and rightsizes in order to deal with a changing environment. If possible, however, it avoids fundamental change.

Thus, the synthetic perspective focuses on reengineering the company. The goal will be to eliminate or streamline processes to reduce costs in every way possible. A common result is that the company becomes a low-cost producer of high-quality commodity products. Worse yet, it becomes the premier producer of obsolete products. Although cost cutting is often very important, it is not the panacea that a synthetic perspective is likely to lead you to believe.

The organic perspective differs from the synthetic in that individuals see themselves and their company as part of a larger system. Their situation is defined in the context of the environment; it is about relationships within this environment. Their company's actions within this environment are elements of the changing environment. The goal, therefore, becomes one of changing with the system rather than surviving against the system.

This perspective can create difficulties too. First, you no longer can externalize problems and blame the market, government, or corporate parents for unmet expectations. There is no "we" and "they." Second, there is a tension between trying to avoid change and attempting to respond to change. Put simply, when is it appropriate to reorganize what you are doing, and when is it necessary to rethink what you are doing?

Somewhat simplistically, the synthetic perspective dictates avoiding fundamental change by various control mechanisms, including redesign. Basically, you try to maintain the old situation as long as possible. In contrast, the organic perspective assumes that change is fundamental and dictates mechanisms for adapting to change. In other words, you try to anticipate possible new situations and adapt to the environment within which these situations are emerging. The synthetic perspective assumes that you are in control or at least that control is an ultimate objective. You have the power and responsibility to make things the way they should be. The organic perspective, in contrast, is premised on the necessity of collaborating with other elements of your environment. You have the power and responsibility to adapt to the evolving environment, of which you are a part. This adaptation involves collaboration for mutual benefit rather than control to gain advantage.

Fundamental change does not occur without relinquishing complete control and relying on collaboration to create and pursue new situations. However, with the synthetic perspective, there is substantial risk that command and control will be substituted for vision and leadership. In such situations, the need to change usually results in more assertive command and control rather than reconsideration of basic assumptions.

The organic point of view provides a better basis from which to deal with fundamental changes in relationships with markets. It is much more attuned to the environment and a company's role within the environment. Thus, it provides a better framework for tracking and understanding trends and events.

As indicated earlier, a company's perspective creates a fundamental difference in its expectations about responses to changing situations. The synthetic company reorganizes and reengineers to become what top management has chosen to be. The organic enterprise adapts to external and internal forces and trends, becoming, in effect, what the environment wants it to be.

Which perspective is better? It depends on the situation. If the assumptions underlying the current situation remain valid—or can be updated—and the changes to which management aspires are achievable, then the synthetic point of view can be very powerful. In contrast, if assumptions are substantially off and the old situation no longer matches reality, the organic perspective is more useful.

Put simply, if management wants to transform an armadillo into an antelope, the organic perspective provides a more realistic basis for decision making. The synthetic point of view implies that the armadillo can be disassembled—its parts and genetic code restructured—and then reassembled as an antelope. The organic model argues against this possibility because the whole armadillo would have to be dealt with—its biology, psychology, sociology, culture, and so on. Thus the organic perspective provides a more realistic basis from which to pursue fundamental change.

Balancing Synthetic and Organic Perspectives

A key aspect of strategic thinking is balancing the two perspectives. The appropriate balance of synthetic and organic points of view varies depending on the nature of the ten common situations that the company finds itself in and, thus, on the differences in its relationships with its markets. Distinctions among these situations and relationships provide clear guidance for balancing synthetic and organic perspectives.

For companies in vision quest and evolution situations, the relationship with the marketplace is nascent at best. If they respond organically to market cues at this point, they are likely to give up and do something else. However, if they feel that their passion, persistence, and patience will enable them to gain a good relationship, then their chances of success increase substantially. Thus, in these situations it is useful to adopt a synthetic point of view.

Companies in crossover and crossing the chasm situations need to pay more attention to market cues. Although they have not yet been embraced by the marketplace, there is usually some warming to their offerings. Moving a bit away from the synthetic and toward the organic is likely to help with this transition, although it may not be absolutely necessary.

The steady growth situation presents companies with a dilemma. At this point, the market loves what the company has to offer. It can sell as much as it can produce. A synthetic point of view will work quite well at this point. For example, there is a natural tendency to focus solely on extending and improving internal processes to accommodate increasing demand. Unfortunately, total investment of a company's energies in this way will not prepare it for the situations that follow.

With the consolidation situation, the marketplace begins to set the tone. It now becomes important to think organically about the company's position among the players. It may be much better, for example, to be acquired under attractive terms than to be thwarted in all attempts to acquire others.

With the silent war and paradigm lost situations, a company's position in the marketplace becomes increasingly tenuous. It needs to focus on the nature of the environment and to find new roles, paradigms, and competitive advantages in a marketplace that is not necessarily interested in what it might want to do from a synthetic standpoint. If the synthetic perspective dominates at this point, the company's demise is a distinct possibility.

When a company is in commodity trap and process situations, the marketplace is firmly in charge. There are lots of places to get what it wants. The competition to be the lowest-price, highest-quality producer becomes increasingly heated. A company's ability to understand the nature of the market environment—the organic perspective—is now key to its success, perhaps even to its survival.

As I emphasized in Chapter Two, the ten common situations focus on relationships with the marketplace. Hence, they tend to be affected by issues such as external trends and events, strategic market assumptions, and market opportunities and threats. These issues should be dealt with from an organic perspective. Addressing such issues from a synthetic point of view is very likely to lead to problems, much as it has for the defense companies that have tried to change markets without changing themselves.

Once an issue is addressed and the way to resolve it is clear, the emphasis shifts to plans and programs. Primary concerns become implementation, results, resources, constraints, consequences, demands, and problems. These types of concerns are only meaningful through a synthetic point of view. Although priorities among these concerns should be strongly influenced by the organic perspective, the eventual goal is to synthesize means for dealing with concerns.

Doing all this sounds much simpler than it actually is. Responding organically to external organic forces may require synthesizing plans and programs that are incompatible with the inherent nature of an enterprise. I frequently encounter companies that know that their situation has changed and that their relationship with the market should change accordingly. However, they find that their employees have great difficulty learning to think in terms of outsourcing, third-party sales channels, and so on.

Nevertheless, the key to enabling stable transitions and maintaining stability involves balancing the organic and synthetic perspectives. IBM's formative years (see Chapter Six) provide a good example. IBM responded organically to long-term market trends by synthetically developing a strategy to help its customers deal successfully with the trends that were affecting them. That is, IBM had a deep understanding of the data processing situations that customers faced, and it provided a total package of products and services to help them deal with these situations.

More recently, IBM's nature has limited its ability to respond to market changes. Customers no longer want monolithic solutions. They want to mix and match alternative elements of solutions. They are very sensitive to the prices of all of these elements. IBM's total solution became much too expensive. The skills and infrastructure developed to provide such solutions shifted from being an asset to being a liability. Thus, what was once a strong organic response to market needs atrophied and was no longer organically relevant to the current market.

The need for balance between synthetic and organic perspectives can be illustrated by using a vehicle as an analogy for an enterprise. Navigation, guidance, and control of a vehicle are analogous to strategic, tactical, and operational levels in an enterprise. Navigation involves choosing the routes that are determined by the nature of the environment. Guidance involves balancing outside forces with internal capabilities to assure appropriate paths along the routes. Control focuses on accelerating, braking, turning, and so on, which involve actions that are internally synthesized.

In the context of this analogy, the balance between synthetic and organic is obvious. Seldom do people become so preoccupied with control that they forget to navigate, that is, forget to go where they want to go. However, such a case is not unusual when it comes to companies. A common source of the difficulty involves the care and maintenance of a type of vehicle—that is, a type of company—that is of decreasing relevance in the changing terrain of the marketplace.

Limits to Change

To summarize briefly, a synthetic perspective is powerful when the status quo model is close enough to the reality of the market that fine-tuning is enough to deal with discrepancies. In contrast, when a new corporate model is needed, an organic perspective is much more productive. Some situations may be such that the necessary new model is so different from the old model that adaptation can be very difficult.

Chapter Five describes failures to adapt by automobile and aircraft companies. U.S. automobile manufacturers had great difficulty adapting to quality production of small cars. Ford's adaptation was precipitated by a crisis, while General Motors (GM) has yet to adapt fully. Why? A reasonable conjecture is that Ford's culture was more adaptable—once there was no longer a Ford running the company—than GM's culture, which CEO Sloan had so pervasively changed.

Automobile manufacturers are increasingly caught in commodity trap situations leading to process situations with a focus on quality and process innovations to decrease costs. Escaping these situations is likely to require the realization that a paradigm lost situation has been playing in the background and that a new vision quest or crossover is needed.

Specifically, automobile companies need to recognize that an aerodynamic body, four wheels, and a drive train are no longer the best way to differentiate their vehicle from those of their competitors. For a period, computer control of the engine, environment, and so on provided a competitive advantage. But today virtually every car has these things. Antilock brakes and dual airbags provided a brief advantage, but these too were quickly adopted by all automobile manufacturers.

My conclusion, based on my work with companies in the industry, is that the likely new competitive paradigm will involve providing more value directly to the driver. This kind of value comes from information and aiding systems that support both driving the car and decision making. The key enabling technology for this paradigm change will be software in general and intelligent systems software in particular.

The key question is: Which automakers will make substantial profit margins on this software and which will make very modest profit margins on the commodity-like aspects of cars? I expect that automobile companies will have great difficulty transitioning to software from hardware cultures. Those who adapt most quickly, or find the right alliance partners, will transition quickly from paradigm lost to vision quest situations. Subsequently, because of their huge market bases, they are likely to cross the chasm and experience steady growth fairly quickly.

The aircraft industry faces a similar situation. As discussed more fully in Chapter Five, the U.S. aircraft industry was slow in shifting paradigms to jet engines for military aircraft. Douglas Aircraft was slow in responding to opportunities for commercial jets. It could be argued that Douglas has never fully recovered from this hesitancy of forty years ago. My perception is that the aircraft industry today is caught in a commodity trap situation. All the airlines offer basically the same seat and service. Price is the dominant issue. Consequently, all the airlines and all the aircraft manufacturers are focused on reducing costs.

The paradigm lost situation that is currently playing out involves the old paradigm—that airline passengers buy use of airplane seats for the time it takes to get from point A to point B. The new paradigm assumes that passengers are buying use of a range of capabilities for a period of time. The seat has become a commodity but the other capabilities can provide substantial competitive advantages. These capabilities include entertainment, information, communication, and computation. The airline with the best of these capabilities will attract the most business passengers. Although these kinds of passengers are in the minority, they provide the majority of profits. One airline with which I have worked told me that 10 percent of its passengers—the business passengers—provide 90 percent of its profits.

These types of capabilities are very much software-intensive, much like those just noted for automakers. However, aircraft companies are just as hardware-oriented as automobile companies are. It is not certain that their cultures can adapt. Can they accept the fact that the airplane, like the automobile, has become a commodity-like cabinet for a computer? Can they shift from begrudging the paradigm lost to pursuing aggressively a new vision quest?

Chapter Six discusses these questions as they apply to the computer industry. When the computer industry emerged, Remington-Rand and later General Electric (GE) and RCA were unable to establish and maintain strong market positions. Remington-Rand had an early lead but failed to take advantage of it. GE and RCA later tried to catch up but eventually abandoned this goal.

These three companies were unable to become computer companies. They were already in many other businesses and the nature of these businesses strongly influenced their perspective, working against their establishing themselves as computer companies. Their very natures severely hindered their ability to synthesize what was needed by the organic nature of the marketplace.

More recently I have experienced repeated instances of computer companies struggling with paradigms lost. Computer hardware, especially at the low end of the market, has become a commodity. Functionality has become standardized and price is the dominant competitive issue. As a result, profit margins have continually shrunk. Margins on software, in contrast, have remained good. The obvious conclusion is that computer manufacturers should provide more value through software. I have been in numerous strategy discussions with computer companies where this conclusion was reached.

Yet while these companies agree with this conclusion, they have great difficulty adopting this strategy. Almost all of their decision making is dominated by one overriding goal—bending metal. Most of their processes and infrastructures were designed and refined to create and manufacture large volumes of hardware. When it comes to the culture and infrastructure necessary for creating software, they are at a competitive disadvantage.

Without doubt, defense companies, described in Chapter Seven, provide the best examples of limited ability to change. The nature of defense companies is highly attuned to dealing with one customer, pushing technology, and avoiding risks. This nature severely limits their abilities to synthesize major changes.

Furthermore, the distributed, multifaceted nature of the defense organism, which includes industry, government, and academia, makes it very difficult to synthesize new approaches. For example, government programs that encourage companies to shift to commercial markets do not consider the fact that these companies' primary relationships have been with government procurement organizations, government laboratories, and to some extent university laboratories. Yet all of these players are affected by trends in defense spending and in varying ways all have to participate in the defense industry's transition.

To a great extent, enterprises such as GM, IBM, and the Department of Defense have been trapped by their successes. They became highly specialized and very successful at operating within particular paradigms. Indeed, they became so successful that they forgot about the possibility that another paradigm might emerge. When new paradigms inevitably did emerge, these massive enterprises had institutionalized the old paradigms to a such an extent that they could not recognize, much less respond to, the changes. Although these enterprises may recover from these setbacks, they will never regain the dominant positions they once enjoyed.

Correlates of Successful Change

At this point, readers may find it increasingly clear that companies need to make the transition to new situations. At the same time, they may think it increasingly unlikely that companies can succeed in doing so. This may be true in general. Certainly, history supports such a conclusion. However, I do not think that it has to be true in particular. I am convinced that individual firms can successfully anticipate, recognize, and respond to changing relationships with their markets.

There are five correlates of successful transitions. These correlates are derived to a great extent from the case histories presented in Chapters Five through Seven. I summarize them here:

1.   The first correlate is leadership, that is, management commitment to new vision quest or crossover situations. The quest cannot simply be a tactic for shoring up sagging sales. It has to represent a compelling desire to add value to the market in new and specific ways.

2.   The second correlate concerns knowledge of markets and the innovation processes necessary for crossing the chasm. Management must be committed to gaining the knowledge and skills that will enable the company to become a new company. The goal is not just to change markets but also to change the company.

3.   The third correlate involves identifying and facilitating crossover of key enabling technologies and processes. Success is likely to depend on crossing over to new markets with a few key things, not a lot of baggage. Thus, much of the old company—including many of its employees—is unlikely to cross over.

4.   The fourth correlate also involves crossover. In this case, it relates to crossovers originating in areas other than within a company. Acquisitions of key individuals and technologies, as well as whole firms perhaps, may be needed to create the critical mass necessary for successful transitions.

5. The fifth correlate of success is management and investor patience and persistence, that is, often a wait of five or more years for profits. To achieve this kind of patience, there must be buy-in to an evolution situation and recognition that the new venture will not quickly replace falling sales in the traditional businesses.

If one or more of these five correlates is absent, a company is likely to find itself in a consolidation situation. In that case, the goal is either to be one of the surviving players or to find the most profitable way to leave the market. Often, the only reasonable option is to focus on successfully transitioning to a process situation.

The biggest factor that works against these five correlates of success is obvious and often overwhelming: time. By the time companies recognize the need to respond to the market, they usually have little time left before their resources are depleted. They often need to transition successfully and profitably to a new situation in six months to a year. This is usually impossible to do.

Why does this happen? Why do companies wait so long? One reason is the common human tendency to become trapped by the details of the current situation. Another reason is the also-common tendency to assume continuity, to believe that the future will be very much like the past. Finally, people usually do not know how to deal with issues of the future. Chapter Four looks at ways to overcome these natural tendencies.

Summary

This chapter has shown how patterns of business situations or relationships with markets create stories. It offered five illustrative stories. Three of them—the classic life cycle, false start, and death spiral—have a variety of undesirable characteristics. Two of them—reinventing the company and branching and pruning—are very attractive.

Unfortunately, companies cannot simply decide to live out the more attractive stories. They cannot easily make changes of such broad scope. Instead, they need to focus on the situations that the stories comprise. They must learn to anticipate, recognize, and respond to potential situations. To the extent that they become skilled at doing this, they will create successful stories.

One of the necessary skills is the ability to balance synthetic and organic perspectives. Companies need to learn when the control inherent in a synthetic perspective works well and when the collaboration necessary in an organic perspective works better.

4

Assessing Your Relationship with the Market

The Situation Assessment Method

The first three chapters of this book discussed common business situations, patterns of business situations, and ways in which these patterns create stories. In this chapter, all of these concepts are brought together to develop the situation assessment method. This method will allow you systematically to assess and monitor your relationships with your markets. It will also help you create the relationships you want while avoiding undesirable ones.

It is useful to begin this chapter by reviewing the earlier discussion of why situation assessment is so important. Two sets of circumstances are likely to lead companies to pursue strategic thinking in a serious way. Both involve fundamental change. The first set involves unavoidable change, such as a rapidly disappearing market. The second concerns compelling opportunities to change, such as new technologies that are on the verge of substantially altering the marketplace.

If companies recognize that they are encountering or are about to encounter one or both of these sets of circumstances, and if they then pursue strategic thinking, they are likely to think deeply about their relationships with the marketplace. Thus, they are likely to plan in the fullest sense of the term.

In contrast, if they do not recognize the existence or probable emergence of such circumstances, they are likely to assume that next year will be very much like last year. They may project a little growth or even a little decline. These projections are usually based on the implicit assumption that their relationships with the marketplace will continue as in the past. These enterprises do not plan. They may budget and call it planning, but it really isn't. They may create impressive financial models and forecasts, but they will not explicitly consider how they are going to maintain their relationships with the marketplace or foster new relationships. They may debate and choose among alternative marketing and sales tactics, but they will not be thinking strategically.

I often see strategic plans that primarily include projections of sales, costs, and profits. The weak link in these projections is the sales projections. The salespeople are told to go out and "make their numbers" even though such plans seldom reflect any serious thinking about how these numbers can be made. Then, when sales goals are not met, profits disappear because costs are often locked in regardless of sales. In such situations, I have often heard astute observations such as, "They could have been profitable if they had maintained their market share" or "Our costs would be fine if sales were just higher."

These superficial observations fail to deal with the real problems. *Why* couldn't the company maintain market share? *Why* aren't its sales higher? The reason is seldom a lack of intention or desire; it is almost always much more fundamental. It usually involves a lack of understanding of the market situation that the company is in or soon will be in. The solution to the problem, therefore, involves the ability to assess situations.

It is particularly critical to be able to assess situations when a company is in circumstances that portend fundamental change. In either set of circumstances, an enterprise wants to create a different company, at least in terms of its relationships with its markets. The company may know exactly the relationship that it seeks. It may know where it wants to be. But how is it going to get there? To answer this question, it must know where it is. To do this, it is essential to assess the situation.

The Situation Assessment Method

Figure 4.1 outlines the situation assessment method. It involves asking three broad questions:

- What is the situation?
- How is the situation likely to unfold?
- Which situation should be pursued?

These questions involve assessment, planning, and commitment, respectively. They involve thinking strategically about where you are, where you might choose to go, the consequences of both, and the value of these consequences.

The first step is to compare marketplace signals with situation indicators to determine probable current and future situations. The result of this comparison is usually several possibilities, particularly for future situations. It is good to have several alternatives at this point because subsequent questions are likely to make one or more of them unattractive.

Let's return to our example of the travel planning software business. If you were in this business, you might want to know if you were still in a steady growth situation. Consideration of this question might lead you to ascertain that it is possible that silent war or paradigm lost situations are emerging. For instance, perhaps you are facing low-cost, offshore competition or changing software paradigms as a result of networking.

Several companies with which I have worked in the computer industry would have done well to consider such possibilities. However, as Chapter Six discusses, many computer companies do not. They assume that steady growth is their manifest destiny and that their dominant paradigm is unassailable. This assumption is not explicit but implicit in their corporate culture. A rude awakening is required in order for this assumption to be questioned.

The second step in the situation assessment method is to consider the implications of the likely situations by drawing upon the

FIGURE 4.1. The Situation Assessment Methodology.

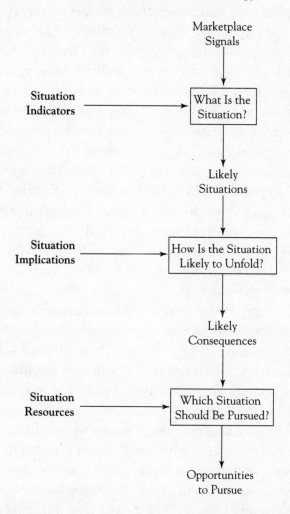

concepts presented in Chapter Two. Doing this allows for anticipation of the probable consequences of different situations. In thinking about these implications, you should transform the general phrasing of implications in Exhibit 2.1 to context-specific wording for your company.

For example, if you were in the travel planning software business you would consider the consequences of being in steady growth, silent war, or paradigm lost situations. What would you expect to happen if these situations persisted or emerged? How would you deal with the consequences, both externally (in the marketplace) and internally (within your company)? How would you sell both customers and employees on the changes that might be necessary? Try to generate context-specific answers to these questions, using Exhibit 2.1 to prompt your thinking.

One reason why the computer companies with which I worked did not entertain alternative solutions was that they could not deal with their implications. They could not face the necessity of outsourcing manufacturing when they considered "bending metal" to be a core competency. They could not face the fact that hardware was becoming a commodity and software the high-margin part of the system when they had always practically given away the software in order to sell the hardware. They could not sell the necessary changes to either the employees or themselves. Yet the market was quite ready for these changes.

The third step in the situation assessment method is to evaluate the desirability of the consequences considered in step two as well as the resources required to pursue these situations. This evaluation influences the choice of opportunities to pursue. At this point, the number of alternatives usually becomes quite constrained, often reduced to just one or two opportunities.

Thus in your travel planning business you might compare the consequences of sticking with steady growth assumptions rather than investing in changing software paradigms. It is quite likely that the technology investment required for new software paradigms would be substantial, as would be the risk that you could not catch the other players in the market. You might also have difficulty getting your organization to buy into the investment. Thus, you might consider instead starting a networked products division, investing a reasonable but modest amount in its development, and locating it somewhere remote from the current business.

This approach has been adopted by computer companies as they dealt with potentially changing situations. It certainly can succeed. However, it often fails. A common problem is the exercise of too much control by the corporate parent as well the imposition of too many financial and cultural burdens. Corporate parents are so concerned that the fledgling venture will fail that they smother it with attention.

What if the constraints imposed in step three are such that there are no alternatives? This may imply that the changes needed are much more fundamental than anticipated. In this case, you may have to entertain vision quest, evolution, or crossover situations that you might not have originally thought reasonable. It may also imply that you cannot change in the ways that you think necessary. (This possibility is pursued in greater depth in Chapter Eight.)

Thus, each of the three questions delineated in Figure 4.1 leads to several more detailed questions. Exhibit 4.1 lists these more detailed questions in checklist form.

Before considering these more detailed questions, it is important to think about the object of the assessment. Specifically, to what entity or entities does it apply? If your strategic planning focuses on the company as a whole, you will probably want to answer the questions for your whole company. For example, you will want to consider the relationship your company as a whole has with the marketplace. In contrast, your planning may place emphasis on product lines, with the overall strategy being a composite of the individual product line strategies. In this case, you will want to answer the situation assessment questions for each product line. Smaller companies usually answer the questions for the company as a whole whereas larger companies frequently answer them for each product line. The latter strategy is particularly useful when the goal is to create a portfolio of relationships with markets. Such a portfolio may enable a company to harvest profits from one situation while investing in another.

What Is the Situation?

To answer the first question, begin by asking, "What did I think the situation was?" In other words, pick one or more of the ten common situations or assign probabilities to each of the ten situations.

Doing this may be more difficult than it seems. People are quite proficient at deluding themselves. Perhaps they remember the

EXHIBIT 4.1. The Twenty Questions in Situation Assessment.

What Is the Situation?

☐ 1. What did I think the situation was?
☐ 2. What has happened or is happening?
☐ 3. Is the situation consistent with what I thought it was?
☐ 4. Do I want or need the two situations to be consistent?
☐ 5. What are the costs of recognizing the changed situation?
☐ 6. What is the new or modified situation?
☐ 7. What do I want it to be?
☐ 8. Can I accept ambiguity?

How Is the Situation Likely to Unfold?

☐ 9. How has the situation unfolded in the past?
☐ 10. How do I want or hope it will unfold?
☐ 11. What factors mitigate for or against its likely unfolding?
☐ 12. How will I know if the situation is unfolding as expected or needed?
☐ 13. Can I accept ambiguity?
☐ 14. Can I support or rationalize my expectations?

Which Situation Should Be Pursued?

☐ 15. Are the consequences desirable or acceptable?
☐ 16. Can they be advocated or defended?
☐ 17. What are the likely benefits, costs, risks?
☐ 18. Will my organization buy in or perform?
☐ 19. What if it fails?
☐ 20. How might the situation go wrong?

steady growth of five years ago. Are they discounting the significance of setbacks in recent years? Maybe they feel that they crossed the chasm when they made their second sale. The situation assessment method is likely to correct these kinds of misperceptions.

After you've determined your *assumed* situation, look at the signals you are getting from the marketplace and ask, "What has happened or is happening?" Start with the indicators discussed in Chapter Two and outlined in Exhibit 2.1. In addition, the list of forty-one indicators shown in Exhibit 4.2 may help you in this process.

EXHIBIT 4.2. Indicators of the Common Situations.

Indicator/Situation	VQ	EV	CO	CC	SG	CS	SW	PL	CT	PR
Missionary zeal	P	L								
Strong commitment	P	L								
Mixed signals	P	L								
Ahead of times	P	L								
Missed development targets		P	L	L						
Missed sales targets		P	L	L						
Compatibility problems		P	L	L						
Market skepticism		P	L	L						
Perceptions of risk		P	L	L						
Missing technologies or processes	L	P	L	L						
Limited key technologies or processes	L	P	L	L						
New domain unaware	L	P	L	L						
Sales to innovators	L		P	L						
Sales to early adopters	L		P	L						
Difficulty with pragmatists	L		P	L						
Lack of whole product	L		P	L						
Sales volume				P	L	L				
Market share				P	L	L				
Profits				P	L	L				
Technology acceptance				P	L	L				
Production learning curve				P	L	L				

(exhibit continued on next page)

Exhibit 4.2. (cont.)

Indicator/Situation	VQ	EV	CO	CC	SG	CS	SW	PL	CT	PR
Number of players						P	L	L	L	
Market share scramble						P	L	L	L	
Price pressures						P	L	L	L	
Increased marketing and sales costs						P	L	L	L	
Decreased margins						P	L	L	L	
Few discretionary resources						P	L	L	L	
Potential new players							P	L	L	
Potential new technologies							P	L	L	
Technologies mature in other domain							P	L	L	
Technology obsolescence	L		L					P		
Unmet expectations	L		L					P		
Lack of improvements	L		L					P		
All products similar					L	L			P	L
Quality, service, price central					L	L			P	L
High marketing and sales costs					L	L			P	L
Deep discounts					L	L			P	L
Low margins					L	L			P	L
Industry standards					L					P
Cost pressures					L					P
Financial performance focus					L					P

Note: P refers to present indicators, L to leading indicators.

Exhibit 4.2 shows both present and leading indicators. As their names suggest, *present indicators* relate to current situations while *leading indicators* relate to future situations. To illustrate how Exhibit 4.2 is used, consider the indicators toward the bottom of the figure. Look at the five indicators starting with "all products similar" and ending with "low margins." If, according to the market signals, these indicators are strong, then there is a strong present indicator of a commodity trap situation. There are also strong leading indicators of process, steady growth, and consolidation situations. In other words, the company is probably in a commodity trap situation with strong a possibility that process, steady growth, or consolidation situations will emerge.

Acknowledgment of these indicators would probably lead a company to pursue a branching and pruning story (see Chapter Three for a detailed discussion of this strategy). In particular, it would likely pursue the sequence commodity trap–process–steady growth. The decision to do this would depend, however, on the amount of support for the other indicators shown in Exhibit 4.2.

How do you determine the presence or absence of indicators? I suggest that everyone on the top management team anonymously rate these indicators. They may use a simple rating scale of high, medium, or low, or a numerical scale of 1 to 10. As noted earlier, these ratings may be determined for the company as whole or for different product lines or divisions.

There are several ways to combine the individual ratings into a composite rating for each indicator. Averaging the responses is reasonable, although one extreme response can skew the average. Using the median response of team members avoids this problem. It is also sometimes a good idea to use the best ratings or worst ratings as the composite ratings to get a sense of best- and worst-case assessments.

When the perceptions of members of the management team are collected and averaged, conflicting perceptions are likely to be expressed. It is typical for conflicts to occur across functional areas. For example, engineering and marketing may disagree about whether development targets are being missed. Engineering may claim that the targets were unrealistic while marketing asserts that the technology is far less mature than engineering believed.

The ensuing discussions on this point and others are healthy and important elements of strategic thinking. The situation assessment method can help to raise and clarify such conflicts. Once these conflicts are discussed, it is usually possible to reach consensus, if not complete agreement, on the extent to which each of the indicators is present or absent.

In sum, I suggest that the members of the top management team independently rate the presence of each of the forty-one indicators shown in Exhibit 4.2. In addition, it is helpful to employ the median of these ratings for answering the rest of the twenty assessment questions listed in Exhibit 4.1. As you become more familiar with the overall method, you can employ some of the variations discussed in the preceding paragraphs.

As a result of this process, the third question shown in Exhibit 4.1 is asked: "Is the situation consistent with what I thought it was?" To answer the question, compare the indicators just identified as present or absent with those previously believed to reflect the situation, that is, the a priori situation. Doing this sounds easy: you need simply compare the strength of support for the a priori situation with the strength of support for others. However, related questions may cause you to refine your initial answers.

One related question is, "Do I want or need the two situations to be consistent?" A relatively new venture, for example, may not want to seek complete consistency between expected situations and situations with strong indicators. In other words, when a company is just getting started it is likely to be more than willing to accept discrepancies as indications that the a priori assessment is wrong relative to the identified indicators. Such mistakes are, of course, much easier to deal with early on.

Another related question is, "What are the costs of recognizing that the situation has changed?" This question should get management to consider the implications of advocating or announcing that the assumed situation is not the actual situation. In my experience, it is important to anticipate probable reactions to such conclusions.

In other words, how will people react when you assert that the commonly accepted situation is no longer true—perhaps no longer relevant? They are likely to ignore you because they do not want to believe you. They will shoot the messenger if they can. If you are the boss, you may avoid the bullets but not the skepticism. (Chapters Five through Seven present numerous examples of this phenomenon.)

However, the reaction will be more constructive if you have already considered the next question: "What is the new or modified situation?" To a great extent, this question can be answered with the help of Exhibit 4.2. However, if there are many relevant indicators and possible situations, you may want to weed out the alternatives. Several alternative methods are discussed later in this chapter.

Of course, beyond dealing with indicators and probabilities, there is also the issue of desirability. Management cannot choose the new situation or situations without considering the nature of the enterprise that it is asking for support. Put simply, you need to understand what you can sell to your partners, colleagues, employees, and so on.

Thus, the possibility of a new situation or situations almost always begs the question, "What do I want it to be?" Is the new situation good news or bad news? Does it reflect progress or a setback in pursuing the company's mission? The answer to this question will obviously affect the explanation given to others for the conclusion that the situation is in the process of changing or has already changed.

Good news in general can be bad news in particular. For example, a great new opportunity may propel the company forward through a crossover situation that requires only a subset of all the skills that once were of central importance. Obviously, this opportunity is not likely to result in universal enthusiasm. Nevertheless, this opportunity may be exactly what the company needs if it is not to fade into much less desirable situations.

Another important question is, "Can I accept ambiguity?" It is quite possible—and in fact very likely—that the process of situation assessment will lead a firm to entertain a much wider range of situations than might have been anticipated. This is because the market signals may contain very mixed messages. In other words, some indicators will strongly support one situation while other indicators will strongly support others. This is particularly true during times of substantial change.

Although the ambiguity will work itself out if the indicators continue to be monitored, there remains the fundamental problem that a company has to act, not just observe. This may require multiple plans or plans with contingency points related to alternative resolutions of the ambiguity. This can be a frustrating process. Nevertheless, skill in successfully entertaining multiple situations simultaneously can help a company become very agile.

At this point, the set of feasible current and future situations has been identified. Feasibility in a broad sense can be determined by using the indicators in Exhibit 4.2 for guidance. Feasibility in a narrow sense must be determined by taking into account the nature of the individual company, including its competencies and culture.

How Is the Situation Likely to Unfold?

Now that the feasible set of situations—one or more current situations as well as alternative potential future situations—has been determined, the obvious interest will be in how they are likely to unfold. To make this determination, a good starting point is to ask, "How has the situation unfolded in the past?" This question can be answered in several ways.

First, if you have been through this situation before, you are likely to have strong context-specific experiences that you can draw upon. Second, you can use the knowledge of typical implications of the common situations as compiled in Exhibit 2.1. Third, you can refer to industry-specific information such as that presented in Chapters Five through Seven for the transportation, computer, and defense industries. All in all, there is usually a rich set of data and knowledge to call upon once you recognize that a particular situation has emerged or is likely to emerge. This is one of the primary reasons for making situation assessment a central element in strategic thinking.

Of particular importance in this process is consideration of past experiences. What successes did the company experience in the past and, specifically, why did they happen? Past successes are sometimes much less the result of plans and skill than many may be willing to admit. Often, the big kill just wanders into the backyard, trips over the gun, and shoots itself. The hunters then run out and celebrate their great skill. Lack of sustained success may be the result of the serendipitous nature of the initial success. The problem with this is not the serendipity but the failure to recognize it.

In the process of considering how situations have unfolded in the past and how they might unfold in the future, you should also ask, "How do I want or hope it will unfold?" For example, let's say you are firmly in the midst of a consolidation situation. What do you want to happen? Do you want to sell out for the best price? Or do you want to be one of the acquirers? Although you may not be able to influence which situation emerges, you often can decide what role you want for yourself within it.

It is interesting how often people work backwards from what they imagine to be possible. Where I ask, "What do you want?" they ask, "What can I achieve?" Feasibility is irrelevant at this point; desirability is the issue. Yet many people, even CEOs and other top executives, are unwilling to let themselves desire things that they are not sure they can attain. This is not the best mind-set with which to approach strategic thinking.

You can use Exhibit 2.1 to help you in this process too. Review the implications summarized. Which implications or consequences are most desirable? Are any of them implied by your current situation or likely future situations? Exhibit 2.1 can help prompt your thinking about what you are seeking as well as what you are trying to avoid.

After one considers what is desirable, the question becomes, "What factors mitigate for or against its likely unfolding?" Again, let's say you're in a consolidation situation. What will affect your abilities to be an attractive seller or buyer? To begin, you might consider the indicators associated with consolidation situations as well as the indicators associated with likely transition situations. Then, to the extent possible, try to make yourself attractive in terms of these indicators.

Sometimes people have difficulty focusing on why things may not work out as planned. It is much easier to consider the many reasons why success is likely. However, it is much more useful to plan for contingencies before they arise. It is much more useful to envision problematical circumstances before they become irreversible. Then, when these circumstances actually arise, you will be much more willing to admit that things have gone wrong and adjust your plans accordingly.

As you anticipate how things may unfold, you should also ask, "How will I know if the situation is unfolding as expected or needed?" If you are trying to make yourself an attractive acquisition target, how can you determine if that is happening? Monitoring the indicators in Exhibit 4.2 is a good start. You might also create a special case of the consolidation situation, one where the prime actor gets acquired, and define special cases of the general indicators in Exhibit 4.2. In fact, you should consider defining special cases—special to your context—for all of the relevant indicators. Thus, as you become increasingly familiar with the situation assessment method, you can tailor it to your company.

Figuring out how a situation is unfolding is seldom done as neatly as one would wish. Thus, as with the earlier questions, it is again necessary to ask, "Can I accept ambiguity?" Whereas earlier the ambiguity concerned situations, now it concerns the consequences of situations. For example, if you're in a consolidation situation, can you for a brief period at least act as both a potential seller and a potential buyer? In fact, since you may still be considering multiple types of situations, can you accept this ambiguity too? In general, can you accept ambiguity about both where you are and the consequences of being there?

Of course, even if you have to act in accordance with two or more situations, you will nevertheless form expectations. You are also likely to have to communicate these expectations to your company. Thus a new question becomes necessary: "Can I support or rationalize my expectations?" One of the best ways to gain this kind of support is through the indicators just discussed. In other words, the future may be portrayed in terms of context-specific manifestations of the indicators and implications in Exhibit 2.1, Figure 3.1, and Exhibit 4.2.

Specifically, the situation assessment method itself provides an excellent framework within which to present and defend expectations. The rationale and data driving expectations are clear and auditable. The method also helps you explain why alternative sets of expectations may not make sense.

Which Situation Should Be Pursued?

At this point, you are considering one or more situations. Likely consequences are known and potential roles and the implications of actions have been considered. Choosing among these alternatives involves asking, "Are the consequences desirable or acceptable?"

This question can be answered on several levels, ranging from detailed to broad. Strategies for pursuing a particular situation might be translated into detailed tactical and operational plans which, in turn, may be evaluated in terms of long-term financial returns. Such detailed evaluations are technically feasible. They are also often required by corporate or external investors. Nevertheless, I recommend avoiding this approach if possible.

Why? Quite simply, this is a very time-consuming way to evaluate alternatives. It is much better to proceed more quickly by sacrificing detail. You can rely solely on the knowledge of the situations provided in this book and the context-specific knowledge of your cross-functional team of key managers.

You may find surprising my suggestion that your key managers are important sources of knowledge relevant to fundamental changes of relationships with markets. You may even think that your key managers are the biggest barriers to such changes. Yet I argue that these people are central to situation assessment.

The reason is simply that context-specific interpretations of the elements of the situation assessment method are needed. This book cannot do that for you, but your key managers can provide these interpretations or at least alternative interpretations for the team to debate. The situation assessment method will keep the team from drifting into the common traps because it dictates the questions and the alternatives.

Using Exhibit 2.1, Figure 3.1, and Exhibit 4.2 as guides, you should be able to gain a good sense of the nature of each situation, the organizational resources needed within the context of each, and the consequences of each. This knowledge, combined with the market-specific and company-specific knowledge offered by your team, should enable you to answer the question of desirability and acceptability of consequences.

Thus, you do not need to commission numerous studies and analyze large amounts of data. You can proceed with this fairly broad approach. Once reached, the conclusions of this situation assessment process may serve as the starting point for more detailed types of activities such as scenario analysis. The key is to avoid collecting detailed information about the preponderance of things that simply do not matter.

Beyond deciding whether consequences are desirable and acceptable, you also should ask, "Can they be advocated or defended?" If the extent of the changes envisioned is great, it may be difficult to gain broad support within an enterprise. It is quite possible that the desired changes will encounter barriers because of differing needs and beliefs among the various stakeholders in the enterprise.

One way to make the advocacy process easier is to include more than one advocate. If key managers have been involved in determining and debating consequences, it is likely that this team can be recruited to help with advocacy. In fact, members of this team may be selected on the basis of both their abilities and their inclination to support corporate visions, strategies, and plans.

To advocate and defend the intended changes, another question must be answered: "What are the likely benefits, costs, risks?" This question should be addressed from the perspective of internal stakeholders and focus on the nature and roles of each type of stakeholder. You should consider what each type is likely to gain, lose, and risk in the change process.

The biggest problems are likely to come from stakeholders who feel strongly about the old situation. Their self-images may be totally intertwined with this situation, involving, for example, steady growth in fighter airplane or supercomputer markets. They also may feel very negative about the new situation. If such attitudes are prevalent, a company may have no choice but to entertain also pursuing a crossover situation, as illustrated later in this chapter.

As questions of advocacy, defense, benefits, costs, and risks are answered, the bottom line question may be resolved: "Will my organization buy in or perform?" It will be very difficult and even impossible to accomplish the desired changes if this question cannot be answered affirmatively for at least a core portion of the company. If everyone is going to stand by and watch as one person alone tries to succeed in changing the business, the company is in trouble already.

A large number of passive stakeholders may also dictate the pursuit of a crossover situation. Put simply, it may be necessary to create a new enterprise that only includes actively supportive stakeholders and crosses over a few key people, technologies, and processes. This may sound straightforward but often it is not. As the old situation fades, it may require almost constant attention. As a result, the new fledgling may die in the nest. A firm decision must be made about how to invest attention for the long-term success of an enterprise.

At this point, let us assume that you have successfully advocated and defended the new relationships with your markets and have achieved a reasonable level of organizational commitment. Now you now need to ask, "What if it fails?" In other words, what if many or all of the risks noted come to pass? How can a determination that this has happened be made and what will be done at that point?

For example, a company may be planning a crossover with a key technology to a new market. This can lead to crossing the chasm or, better yet, back to steady growth. (See again Figure 3.1 in Chapter Three.) However, it can also lead to an evolution situation if it is discovered, for instance, that the maturity of this key technology is not yet compatible with the expectations of the new market. At the very least, this would mean a long delay until there is a return on investment. It may mean no return and substantial losses. Can the company deal with such results?

A related question is, "How might the situation go wrong?" In effect, this question concerns the aberrations that might emerge in the transitions that are about to be pursued. The two most frequent possibilities are delayed transition and premature transition. With delayed transition, things progress much more slowly than planned, which is likely to strain resources and threaten continued commitment to the change. With premature transition, in contrast, things happen much more quickly than anticipated. For example, a company briefly crosses the chasm, experiences a short period of steady growth, and then encounters a paradigm lost when there is a sudden technology shift.

Fortunately, the mechanisms within the situation assessment method can help you deal with these contingencies or, at least, track and project changes that may not have been anticipated. In this way, you can regularly update and review your situation assessments. This enables consideration of multiple contingencies in parallel.

This approach also solves another problem: enterprises often agonize over decisions about new situations. They collect endless data and have endless meetings. They are afraid to commit because they know commitment will be expensive and it will take a long time to determine if their decision was wise. But with the approach to situation assessment advocated in this book, companies can commit quickly, monitor progress in a very focused way, and know fairly soon if the commitment needs to be rethought. In fact, this can be done almost continually with, for instance, monthly or quarterly reassessments. In this way, the costs of mistakes are much lower and, therefore, the risks of acting quickly are also much lower.

Updating Assessments

Assessments have a limited "shelf life." Dated assessments can mislead companies into believing that they know what is going on when, in fact, their thinking is stuck in an obsolete situation. Thus, assessments should be updated regularly.

As just indicated, it is best to update quarterly but not more than monthly. Exceptions to this rule of thumb are when events of particular significance occur—for example, a competitor announces a surprise technology breakthrough or there is an important environmental event, such as the sudden tearing down of the Berlin Wall a few years ago. On such occasions, situation assessments should be updated whether or not it is the end of the month or quarter.

Updates may be accomplished in several ways. All involve reference to Exhibit 4.2. Once again, the present indicators are associated with the situation that is presently being experienced while the leading indicators serve as predictors for probable future situations.

Estimates of the presence of some or all of the forty-one indicators shown in the exhibit can be used as a basis for simply inspecting the figure and looking for situations that are strongly supported by the levels of the estimated indicators. A somewhat more formal approach involves assessing indicators on a 3-point or 5-point scale. Sample descriptors are *very low, low, moderate, high, very high*. Using a 1- to 10-point scale is another good way of assessing indicators.

Because each situation is associated with multiple indicators, the strength of support for a situation is calculated based on the number of points it has received, normalized by dividing by the maximum number of points that it could receive. For example,

Exhibit 4.2 shows four indicators primarily associated with the vision quest situation and five associated with the evolution situation. On a 10-point scale, one situation (vision quest, for example) may get as many as forty points while another (evolution, perhaps) as many as fifty. To deal with this disparity, ratings of indicators are summed within each situation and then divided by the maximum number of points possible. Thus, the strength of support for both vision quest and evolution will range from 0.0 to 1.0.

Estimates of the presence or absence of the key indicators are needed in order to determine any of the approaches just described. These estimates can be obtained if each member of the management team independently completes a form that lists the forty-one indicators and also provides space for the individual to explain the basis for his or her estimate. As discussed earlier, estimates may be combined by using either a mean or median—I suggest the median—perhaps weighting each estimate by the credibility of the explanation provided. Also noted earlier, conflicts in estimates are common and often result in fertile discussions that usually lead to consensus.

Bayes' Rule provides another approach to updating assessments in a probabilistic manner. To begin, each situation is assigned an a priori probability—that is, the probability of a situation before taking into account new information. This may be thought of as a conditional probability, which can be expressed as the probability of a situation given all past data as reflected by all past indications.

A new indicator level constitutes a new piece of data, which is likely to cause us to update our probability estimates. Specifically, what now must be determined is the probability of each situation given all past data plus the new piece of data. In other words, how does the probability change when the new piece of data is taken into account?

Many years ago, psychologist Ward Edwards showed that people are not very good at estimating probabilities in this way. But they are pretty good at estimating the probability of the new piece of data occurring, assuming that a situation is happening or about to happen. In other words, people are good at estimating what will happen based on the assumption that a certain situation exists. More technically, they are good at estimating the conditional probabilities of particular indicator levels, given specific situations. In contrast, people are not so good at assessing what situation exists based on a particular event. They are not good at estimating the conditional probability of specific situations, given particular indicator levels. Thus, people are able to estimate conditional probabilities but not the ones that we need.

Fortunately, there is a relationship between these two conditional probabilities. This relationship is called Bayes' Rule, which is defined by the following equation (in which $Prob$ = probability and Sit = situation):

$$\text{Prob (Sit X | New Data)} = \frac{\text{Prob (New Data | Sit X) Prob (Sit X | All Past Data)}}{\sum \text{Prob (New Data | Sit Y) Prob (Sit Y | All Past Data)}}$$

Thus, the probability of a situation given the new data equals the product of the probability of the new data given the situation and the a priori probability of the situation given all previous data, divided by the product of the same two probabilities summed over all possible situations.

Using this rule, new data can be continually processed with each new probability estimate becoming the a priori probability for the next calculation.

There are variations on this process. For example, Bayes' Rule can be modified to utilize likelihood ratios or odds rather than probabilities. This method is helpful for people who are not accustomed to thinking in terms of probabilities. There are also versions based on fuzzy set theory. In this theory, the concept of membership replaces probability. Fuzzy set theory enables use of subjective relationships that do not conform to the laws of probability.

I suggest that updating be approached in a fairly qualitative manner to begin with, perhaps using only Exhibit 4.2 and rating scales. Once you gain confidence in the situation assessment method, the more formal methods may be employed. In this way, you will develop your own intuitions before relying on computer-based models.

Two Case Studies

At this point, the situation assessment method should seem reasonably straightforward. To sum up, there are ten common situations (shown in Exhibit 2.1), a variety of typical transitions between these situations (Figure 3.1), and forty-one indicators of these situations and transitions (Exhibit 4.2). An analysis of this information will provide the basis for addressing three broad questions (Figure 4.1) and twenty specific questions (Exhibit 4.1) that are designed to help assess and monitor a company's relationships with markets.

You may now feel that this approach to situation assessment can provide a variety of interesting insights that will enhance your strategic thinking and the resulting strategic plans. But you may also feel that the approach is still somewhat abstract. The two case studies presented in this section should provide a needed dose of reality.

The first case study deals with a small, growing company and the second with a large, mature company. It should be noted that the case studies are composites of several I have worked with because I cannot divulge the details of any particular company. Thus, the experiences described are real but did not happen at a single company.

The Small, Growing Company

The first case study focuses on a university spin-off that has become a small, growing company. In fact, I have worked with about ten companies of this type.

This company was founded on the basis of a consulting project where engineering skills were provided to design and develop a software system. The company then used a couple of university-generated ideas to win several Small Business Innovation Research (SBIR) contracts from the federal government.

Thus, this company started out as a contract R&D company. The initial senior members of the company were all active or former university faculty members. The idea was that they could rapidly transfer a few emerging technologies developed in academia to applications in complex engineering systems such as airplanes, power plants, and military systems. The firm was in a vision quest situation.

Within a couple of years, the vision quest turned into crossover and evolution situations. Concepts, principles, methods, and tools initially developed in academia crossed over to the company's customers, which included several large defense contractors and government agencies. The R&D contracts from these customers fostered the evolution of these technologies.

The company grew quickly and soon had almost a hundred employees. There was a sense that the chasm had been crossed and a steady growth situation was emerging. However, by the late 1980s the defense market was declining. This trend rapidly accelerated with the fall of the Berlin Wall and events that followed.

The company was not surprised by this decline. Fortunately, based in part on kind of the thinking elaborated in this book, management had foreseen this consolidation. In the mid to late 1980s, they had begun to see indications of consolidation emerge. (See indicators for consolidation situations in Exhibit 4.2.) A scramble for market share had led defense companies to cost-share in order to win R&D contracts. Price pressures and decreased margins became common.

The company was convinced that its steady growth situation could not be sustained. Management also felt that much less desirable situations might soon emerge. By the late 1980s, the firm started to be affected by consolidation. Consequently, management began to anticipate and plan a major transition.

The intention was to cross over technologies and people to applications in manufacturing systems. This choice was strongly affected by recommendations from several industry leaders who felt that the firm's technology would result in innovative applications in this industry. The choice of manufacturing systems was also compatible with the original vision quest. Nevertheless, this choice would result in a new evolution situation.

As efforts in this area progressed, the indicators of an evolution situation became increasingly strong. As the indicators of evolution situations in Exhibit 4.2 would lead one to expect, the company missed sales targets while encountering compatibility problems, market skepticism, and perceptions of risk on the part of manufacturing executives who did not see importing of defense technologies as an opportunity. It did not miss any development targets—because it never secured any development contracts. Its very modest sales were in consulting services.

After a couple of years, it was clear that the evolution situation was going to be a very, very long one. A lack of key indicators for crossing the chasm provided ample evidence of this fact. In particular, the company was not achieving the sales to innovators and early adopters that the indicators in Exhibit 4.2 would lead one to expect. Based on the lack of these indicators, the company shelved its manufacturing systems aspirations.

Management realized that a different transition was needed. In particular, a transition that involved providing a total product rather than something that had to be integrated into a larger system was needed. They wanted to avoid having to depend on knowledge of larger systems and relationships with vendors of these systems.

The company decided to focus on business systems in general and systems for supporting business process planning in particular. This choice was determined by a desire to cross over specific technology for supporting people in designing and redesigning business processes. The firm had deep knowledge in this area based on several R&D contracts where it studied the use of information technology to support business practices.

In contrast to its brief foray into manufacturing systems, management was not trying to cross over the whole company. Only a small set of technologies and competencies were relevant to the business systems domain—and these "few good things" were crossed over. The indicators of crossover situations in Exhibit 4.2—in this case, limited key technologies and processes and a new domain that was relatively unaware of these technologies—provided strong signals.

Thus, the company was back to a crossover situation that soon became yet another evolution situation. Ambitious and optimistic development and sales targets for planning tools and services were not met. Management came to realize that the products, as well as what Moore (1991) calls "the compelling reason to buy," needed time to mature.

The company discovered that business systems customers were primarily interested in having their process planning problems solved. The use of leading edge technologies was of secondary importance. Thus, this company's innovation came in the formulation of planning problems rather than the technologies with which it embodied the planning tools. This was a difficult lesson for many of the more ardent technologists employed by the company.

In the process of learning this lesson, the firm also learned it had lost a paradigm without realizing it. Technology-driven invention was replaced by market-driven innovation. The result was that most of its technologists did not cross over to the business systems market. Most stayed in government contract R&D, the portion of the business that continued to experience a consolidation situation.

The evolution situation within the business systems thrust continued for three or four years, growing much more slowly than they had hoped but nevertheless growing. It became clear that the transition to a crossing the chasm situation would require a focus on changing the customer mix. As indicated in Exhibit 4.2, management needed to find a way to appeal to more pragmatic customers who were unlikely to be interested or intrigued by the company's innovative formulations of planning problems.

The company tried several ways of repackaging its products and services so that they would be viewed as whole products rather than pieces of solutions. The result was a few sales to pure pragmatists. The company also increasingly focused on market segments involving semiconductors, electronics, computers, and communications, as well as other types of technology-oriented companies for which these technologies are central. In this way, as Moore emphasizes, customers in different companies became aware of each other and sales became a bit easier.

This company is still in the process of crossing the chasm today, but glimmers of a steady growth situation have begun to emerge. It has developed multiple sales channels, including direct sales of planning products and services by its own sales forces, third-party sales by value-added resellers who package its products with consulting services, and a nascent catalog sales channel involving both its own catalog and several others. Sales volume is steadily growing. Of particular importance, new versions of products are being developed with more predictable schedules, costs, and quality. Thus, considering the indicators of steady growth in Exhibit 4.2, this company is clearly entering a steady growth situation.

The Large, Mature Company

The preceding case study depicts a very small company. Such companies can entertain a wider range of changes and, in general, make changes more easily than large, mature companies can. Although large companies usually have more resources, they also often must deal with the accumulated inertia that inherently opposes change.

Once again, the following case study is necessarily a composite that reflects many of the companies with which I have worked. Considering the industries emphasized in this book, it should come as no surprise that this composite is drawn from my experiences with automobile, aircraft, computer, and defense companies.

This case study begins at a very different point than that of the first case study. Most of the executives and senior managers within this large company easily recognized many of the indicators in Exhibit 4.2. This mature company had experienced consolidation situations in some form. Silent war situations had affected it. Paradigm lost situations had affected it. Nevertheless, it had survived.

I became involved with the company as it wrestled with commodity trap and process situations. Management was reluctant to agree on the presence of a commodity trap situation. It was very difficult for them to accept that their high-tech products had become commodities. It was also difficult for them to accept that their high-tech engineering expertise was no longer unique.

However, the indicators of a commodity trap situation as shown in Exhibit 4.2 were quite clear, especially the high marketing and sales costs, the necessity of deep discounts to maintain revenues, and consequent lower and lower margins. The strength of these indications was such that executives and managers were willing to entertain, at least briefly, the possibilities of a commodity trap situation.

In contrast to their reluctance to admit the presence of a commodity trap, they quickly recognized the importance of the process situation and were investing substantial efforts in pursuing it. These efforts were prompted, at least in part, by the ubiquity of total quality management and business process engineering. As Exhibit 4.2 would lead one to expect, the company was facing actual or de facto industry standards, constant cost pressures, and an overriding goal of continually increasing financial performance.

The key situation assessment question for this company was whether its ongoing commodity trap and process situations would result in transitions back to the opportunities of steady growth or, instead, to the pressures of consolidation. A question that had not been entertained was where steady growth would lead if the company was fortunate enough to make this transition. As indicated in Figure 3.1 and Exhibit 4.2, the most likely path back was through silent war and paradigm lost.

The realization that most indications portended these types of cyclic transitions led the company to consider how to get ahead of this likely cycle. This desire led to discussions of individual product lines rather than of the whole company. It quickly became apparent that the strengths of indicators varied across product lines. Thus, some product lines were more vulnerable to this cycle than others.

This realization led to discussions of how to deal with threatened product lines. One possibility entertained was simply to let these product lines transition to consolidation situations and, to the extent possible, attempt to maximize the short-term cash flow and long-term acquisition value. In most cases, however, this alternative was viewed as a fallback option. Before committing to this option, substantial effort was invested in exploring possible vision quest, evolution, or crossover situations for these product lines.

The line of reasoning for this exploration was premised on accepting the emerging commodity nature of the core products in the affected lines. The question then became one of determining which innovations could be pursued in order to create high-margin businesses out of what were rapidly becoming low-margin businesses. More specifically, the company looked for ways to break out of the more mature situations (shown toward the bottom of Figure 3.1) and pursue the growth-oriented situations (shown toward the top of the figure).

The companies upon which this composite case study is based responded in different ways. Several of the automobile, aircraft, and computer companies focused on software as a means for adding high-margin functionality to the low-margin hardware that dominated their product lines. In some cases, the goal was to create unique proprietary software technology. In one case, the goal was to bring very high performance, low-cost electronics to a market where this would be a major innovation. In another case, the goal included offering software services to an existing hardware customer base.

One defense company realized, after a year or two of trying, that their product aspirations were inconsistent with their government contracting culture. They recognized that they had long been selling engineering hours rather than products or systems. Subsequently, they focused on providing engineering services to other business units within this large international company.

All of these companies' efforts involved pursuing new situations—usually crossover situations—in parallel with ongoing commodity trap and process situations. The new situations involved just a handful of people, perhaps ten or twenty, who were outside the mainstream of these companies' traditional businesses. In fact, in some cases, these fledgling efforts were intentionally hidden from the rest of the company, or at least isolated, so that they were not affected by the old ways of doing things.

All of these companies discovered how difficult it is to pursue at the same time both mature, high-inertia situations and new, high-velocity situations. The fire fighting that is necessary to maintain the old situations can extinguish nascent situations. The new ventures and their new situations have to be isolated if they are to survive.

The result for these companies was a need for two very different situation assessment processes. These two processes primarily differed in the indicators and implications emphasized. One process monitored the mature situations and the other monitored the fledgling situations, which were not unlike the kinds of situations experienced by the small, growing company described in the first case study.

The greatest tension arose from frequent attempts to judge the fledgling businesses on the same basis as that used for the mature businesses. Although intellectually at least everyone understood the very different nature of the two sets of situations being pursued, it was often difficult for top management to keep this in mind as they responded to developments in the two areas.

In particular, it was difficult for executives and senior managers to keep in mind the five correlates of success discussed in Chapter Three. The factors of which they most easily lost sight was patience and persistence. As most of their business focused on meeting quarterly goals, it was difficult for them to judge new ventures on three- to five-year timescales.

Comparing the Case Studies

It is useful to contrast the ways in which situation assessment worked in the two case studies. For the small, growing company, situation assessment helped management anticipate and recognize situations that were not previously experienced. In contrast, for the large, mature company, the approach allowed management to see in a new light situations that the company had repeatedly experienced.

Most growing companies have little if any experience with true strategic thinking. Hence, asking the twenty questions in Exhibit 4.1 causes them to articulate and debate issues that may not have previously surfaced. Mature companies also seldom think strategically because their existing product lines and day-to-day problems with these product lines tend to dominate their attention. Asking the twenty questions allows them to reconsider a variety of very basic issues that are likely to have been neglected for years.

The situation assessment method allows small companies to act more maturely and to consider systematically business issues that such firms usually avoid. For large companies, the approach helps lessen the stodginess that can come with maturity and helps them act as if they were smaller. Thus, the specific benefits of using this methodology depend on the company's starting point.

The Role of Situation Assessment

Using the situation assessment method in regular discussions about current and probable future situations provides a company with insight into the typical implications of these situations. It also suggests ways in which companies can increase the possibility of desirable situations and decrease the possibility of undesirable situations.

This kind of information can substantially enhance strategic planning in several areas. First, the situation assessment method exposes and helps to systematically explore strategic assumptions. The methodology provides a framework for regularly and easily reviewing assumptions about relationships with the marketplace.

Second, situation assessment complements scenario planning. (See Chapter One for more on this.) It provides a taxonomy of common situations as well as their indications and implications. Scenario planning efforts can begin at this starting point and go on to create versions of these situations that are specific to the industry and company.

Third, and of most significance, the situation assessment method can provide an important context within which to pursue strategic planning. When a company understands its current and likely relationships with its marketplace it can determine what types of plans are needed. For example, if it realizes that its steady growth situation is likely to transition to consolidation, it may consider fostering a crossover situation based on acquiring a new technology from a distant industry. Thus, two plans are needed. Neither of them is the plan that might have been created if the situation had not first been assessed.

Summary

This chapter described a methodology for situation assessment. This methodology can be employed with various levels of formality. Regardless of the level employed, it is very important to keep in mind that you—and not the method or a computer—must perform the situation assessment. The goal is for you to gain insights and ideas about your current and probable relationships with the marketplace. Once you know where you are, you will have the key to getting where you want to go.

5

Transportation

Serving an Existing Market

The history of the transportation industry is in many ways synonymous with the history of the industrialization of the United States. In the early 1800s, the dominant forms of transportation—horse, stagecoach, sailing ship, and so on—had not changed substantially for centuries. Then, within roughly one hundred years, there were steamboats, railroads, automobiles, and aircraft. In the process of moving from stagecoaches and canal boats to jet planes, humankind changed the speed at which it traveled by a factor of a hundred. Trips that once took days now take minutes.

These substantial changes in technology resulted in the formation of thousands of companies. Some prospered briefly. A few prospered for a long period. Only a handful are still with us today. This chapter and the next two chapters explore the nature of this life-and-death phenomenon.

The Steamboat Industry

Robert Fulton is traditionally credited with the invention of the steamboat in 1807. He was fortunate, however, to be able to build on a variety of earlier efforts. The French had experimented with steam-powered boats almost two hundred years before Fulton. In addition, several steamboats were demonstrated following James Watt's improvements of the steam engine in 1775. Fulton had developed a steamboat in France a few years before his unveiling of the *Clermont* in the United States.

The long gestation period for this technology is typical, as the case studies in the next two chapters will illustrate. Indeed, viewed from a broad perspective, these stories reflect evolution rather revolution. Technology slowly matures until someone—usually not the originator, who typically is long gone—is able to transform technological invention to market innovation. Then, growth often occurs quite quickly.

After Fulton's demonstration in 1807, the steamboat industry blossomed. By 1819, a steamboat had sailed from Savannah, Georgia, to Russia. The first all-steam crossing without the use of supporting sails occurred in 1827. By the mid 1800s, transatlantic steamboat lines were competing. For example, the American Collins line, formed to compete with the British Cunard line, temporarily dominated Atlantic trade with its paddle wheelers that could achieve thirteen knots.

The technological push for ever-increasing speeds was a key element of the competition. A particularly important contribution in this regard was the steam turbine, which was patented by Charles Parsons in 1884. Safety was also a critical element of the competition. Although the first iron-hulled boat was demonstrated in Scotland in 1787, it was not until 1850 that iron hulls became predominant. After 1880, steel hulls were dominant. The industry continued to evolve.

But rather than chronicle these general developments, it is more useful to focus on specific market segments and companies. Edwin Dunbaugh in *Night Boat to New England* (1992) provides a rich account of the rise of the steamboat industry for passengers and freight from New York to Providence and Boston, as well as between Massachusetts and Maine. Dunbaugh discusses the many companies formed, the effects of continuing technological changes, and the relationship between the steamboat industry and the development of the railroads.

In 1815, Elihu Bunker's steamer *Fulton* became the first steam-powered vessel in regular service between New York and New

England. By 1822, the success of the New York–Providence route was established. Thus, the industry developed relatively rapidly following the demonstration of the *Clermont* in 1807.

However, competition was constrained as several states granted exclusive rights to specific routes. In 1824, a court ruling stopped this practice. Subsequently, the number of steamboat companies rapidly increased. There was almost constant construction of new vessels, with each competitor trying to gain competitive advantage in terms of travel time. Usually, being 10 percent faster, that is, shaving off one hour in ten, resulted in a gain of significant market share on any particular route.

In 1833, Cornelius and Jacob Vanderbilt entered the competition. Having prospered with steamboats on the Hudson River, the Vanderbilt brothers now focused on Connecticut and steamboat service from New York to New Haven and other Connecticut cities.

Cornelius Vanderbilt played a central role in the development of the transportation industry in the United States. In 1835, he also began competing on the New York–Providence route. He built a much faster boat—the *Lexington*—and was able to offer day service between New York and Boston with twelve and a half hours on the boat and two on the train. By this time, the railroad had replaced the stagecoach as the means to get from the Providence boat landing to Boston. The railroad was faster, more convenient, and more comfortable than stagecoaches.

By the early 1840s, Vanderbilt's apparent intention was to take control of all steamer and rail lines between New York and Boston. He managed to gain complete control of two of the four lines and dominant positions in the other two. But in 1847 he began to extricate himself from these investments, probably because he realized that the competition was rapidly growing. The New York and New Haven Railroad, over which he had no control, was about to open. Vanderbilt was also aware of the emerging formation of the Fall River Line, initially called the Bay State Steamboat Company.

The growth of the Massachusetts textile mills in Fall River, New Bedford, Brockton, and so on prompted the formation of the

Fall River Line. Many other steamboat lines were in existence during this period. Dunbaugh (1992) discusses the Long Island lines— Hartford, New Haven, Stonington—as well as the Providence and Maine lines. Consideration of only one of them—the Fall River Line—is sufficient to illustrate events in this industry.

Like most emerging industries, the steamboat industry experienced both steady growth and consolidation situations, complicated by the fact that the railroads were struggling toward maturity at the same time. In 1854, the Old Colony Railroad acquired the Fall River Line. In 1864, the Fall River Line became the Newport line. In 1869, the Fall River Line was reborn as a merger of the Newport line and the Bristol Line. By this time, it was owned by the Narragansett Steamship Company, top management of which included the legendary Jim Fisk and Jay Gould, who served as president and vice president, respectively. When Fisk was murdered in 1872 by a business associate, Gould became president.

In 1874, the Old Colony Steamship Company was formed as a subsidiary of the Old Colony Railroad. The assets for the new company were purchased from Jay Gould, whose interests had come to be dominated by nonsteamboat matters. By 1879, the Old Colony Steamship Company was prospering: steady growth had emerged yet again. The firm purchased a shipyard in Newport and hired George Peirce, a well-established naval architect from Boston, to manage the Newport yard and design steamers according to the Fall River Line's high standards.

Numerous innovations in steamboat technology were the result of Peirce's tenure during this steady growth situation. In 1883, the *Pilgrim* had a double iron hull segmented in watertight compartments to decrease chances of sinking. The *Pilgrim* was also the first steamer to be lighted throughout by electricity, which was provided by an auxiliary steam generator. The *Puritan* in 1889 was the first steel-hulled steamer built for service on Long Island Sound. The *Plymouth* in 1890 was the first Fall River Line boat to be powered by an expansion-inclined engine rather than a walking-beam engine. The *Priscilla* took her maiden voyage in 1894 with a compound engine. Thus, steady growth enabled one technological innovation after another.

As a result of completion of the New York to New Haven railroad line, the New York and New Haven Railroad pursued a strategy of forcing steamboats off its routes. In response, the Old Colony Railroad, owners of the Fall River Line, acquired the Boston and Providence Railroad in 1888. The goal was to preempt the New York and New Haven from offering New York-to-Boston rail service. A consolidation situation was predominant.

By 1891, three major steamboat lines served New England. Eventually, however, the New York and New Haven with J. P. Morgan on its board took control of all the railroads that owned the steamboat lines. In this way, the company gained control of the steamboat lines. In particular, the New York and New Haven leased the Old Colony Railroad in 1892 and gained effective control of the Fall River Line. By 1898, there were no longer any independent lines. Consolidation in the steamboat market was nearly complete.

By 1889, a through rail route between New York and Boston had been opened. Interestingly, this rail route did not at that time present a serious threat to the established Long Island Sound steamer lines. For a businessman (and most *were* men, in those days) traveling between New York and Boston, the rail trip of five or six hours cost almost a full business day in either direction. Furthermore, he had to pay for a hotel in Boston or New York when he arrived there. But if he took one of the overnight steamers, he could travel between New York and Boston without losing any part of the business day. In addition, the steamer not only provided transportation but also served as a hotel. Thus, by offering a total package of transportation, lodging, and food, the steamers were very competitive. Although railroads dominated the *transportation paradigm*, the steamers dominated the *travel paradigm*.

Dunbaugh (1992) notes that the many steamer lines in New England never seemed able to keep up with increasing demand and technological advances. There was a constant push to outdo one another in speed, safety, and amenities. One can easily imagine those involved in this industry having many late-night discussions analogous to those that are now going on in the software industry about, for example, CD-ROM, multimedia, groupware, networks, and so on.

In other words, a high-tech industry was racing, in the time scale of the era, to put new technologies into use. There were also increasing numbers of players, including railroads, competing for market share. Consolidation resulted as companies gave up or were forced to give up because of meager profits. Yet companies like the Fall River Line found niches where they could still compete, primarily by redefining the paradigm. In fact, the steamer lines were eventually taken over by the railroad companies. Consolidation occurred, therefore, not just within but also across elements of the transportation industry.

Unlike later industries, the steamboat industry does not seem to have proceeded blindly assuming that steamers would always be the preferred transportation choice. In other words, steamboat companies did not experience silent war situations. This was because the railroads matured in parallel with the steamer lines. Thus, the steamboats knew they had no choice but to find a way to compete with the railroads. The railroads, however, never saw the coming impact of the automobile and truck industries. Thus railroad companies did experience silent war situations.

The Railroad Industry

The first reported self-propelled steam vehicle was invented in the late 1600s. Thus, much like the technology for steamboats, this technology exploration process started a long time ago. By the late 1700s, a French-built steam car had been demonstrated in Paris. Soon after, an English-built car was demonstrated. The first practical and successful locomotive was built in Great Britain by John Blenkinsop in 1812.

The railroad industry is usually reported as starting with George Stephenson's creation of the Stockton and Darlington Railway in Britain, which opened in September 1825. Soon after that, it is argued, the railway era really began with the opening of Liverpool and Manchester Railway in September 1830. Thus, once again, maturation of technology to the point of market innovation took close to two hundred years.

Interest in railroads in the United States developed almost as early as it did England. The Baltimore and Ohio Railroad was chartered in February 1827 and began operations in January 1830. The effect of this new transportation technology on stagecoaches and canal boats was felt immediately. Almost overnight, the value of investments in the older technologies decreased substantially. As noted earlier, stagecoach traffic on the Providence-Boston route was effectively eliminated by 1835.

One might think that owners of stagecoach or canal boat companies would have seen this change coming at least five to ten years in advance. However, this was not the case. Railroad travel was initially viewed as noisy and dirty. Consequently, many thought it would never become widespread. This is an archetypical symptom of a silent war situation: competition is acknowledged but discounted. As we know today, such perceptions were very wrong. The speed advantage of rail travel was substantial, and eventually the comfort level was as well.

Alfred D. Chandler in *The Railroads* (1965) and Oliver O. Jensen in *Railroads in America* (1975) chronicle the growth of the railroad industry. Once the mature technology was demonstrated, first in the United Kingdom and soon after in the United States, "railroad fever" became widespread. There was an avalanche of businessmen, speculators, and hawkers of plans, proposals, and prospectuses. By the time that the financial panic of 1837 struck, about two hundred projects were under way. Many of the weaker efforts failed but the railway industry itself grew with abandon.

By the 1850s, the railroad's effects on the American economy were pervasive. Uniform methods of construction, grading, and bridging emerged. Much of the design of rails, locomotives, coaches, and freight cars was close to what we have today, at least in terms of appearance.

A few statistics clearly depict the growth curve of this industry. In 1830, there were only a little over 20 miles of track in the United States; by 1890, there were almost 170,000 miles. In 1840, there were ten locomotive manufacturers; by 1850, there were forty. In 1850, there were roughly twenty-five hundred railway companies; by 1890, there were only about thirty. Clearly, strong growth and the entry of many players were followed by slow growth and consolidation and, consequently, only a handful of players. In retrospect at least, the indicators of the oncoming situations were very clear.

Both Chandler (1965) and Jensen (1975) see the severe economic depression of the 1870s as the dividing line between these periods of American railway history. Coming out of this depression, competition replaced growth as the dominant theme, and dramatic consolidation was the result. Excessive competition in the form of rate wars and reduced revenues drove the consolidation. There were too many players all offering the same services. Therefore, they all had to reduce prices to gain market share. For example, the Pennsylvania system's eight thousand miles in 1893 resulted from consolidation of more than a hundred smaller railroads. Only the fittest—or perhaps the quickest and most savvy—survived.

Growth and subsequent consolidation led to a variety of problems for the bigger lines too. The Santa Fe was one of the biggest lines in the country, with over nine thousand miles in 1890. But the Santa Fe was bankrupt by 1893. Overexpansion in the 1880s and 1890s led to bankruptcy and reorganization for many lines. By the mid 1890s, Chandler reports, a third of the American rail system was involved in foreclosure. Consolidation continued. By 1904 ten broad groups dominated the American rail system. Jensen notes that by 1906 consolidations had organized two-thirds of the system into seven major and several minor systems.

With the railroads the era of big business began in the United States. Vanderbilt, Morgan, Rockfeller, Gould, Pullman, Hill, Drew—these were the names that dominated the period. Political advantage and legislative concessions were sought. Stock manipulations were used to gain control. Large corporations were created and controlled. Jensen notes that at one point eleven partners in J. P. Morgan's firm held seventy-two directorships in forty-seven of the country's largest companies.

The extent of this unregulated power and control began to diminish by 1913 as government regulatory bodies and labor unions began to gain power. In this period the creation of four institutions was completed—large corporations, investment banking houses, regulatory commissions, and labor unions. These institutions soon became integral parts of the American economy.

Although it might be imagined that this institutionalization would bring stability to the transportation industry, continued change was in store. However, at the time, the future of rail transportation looked unlimited. George Hilton explains this point of view in "The Wrong Track" (*Invention & Technology*, 1993). By the early 1900s, urban transportation had been almost completely converted from horses to electric streetcars. The next logical step seemed to be electrification of intercity transport to fill the void between the streetcars and the railroads.

Numerous "interurbans" were built to provide service between the large urban areas and smaller outlying towns and cities. Their attraction was frequency of service, which greatly exceeded the once or twice a day schedule of the railroads. However, interurbans never achieved profitability. They were declining by the end of World War I and had largely disappeared by the onset of the Great Depression.

The interurbans failed because of an unanticipated innovation: the automobile. The impact of the automobile was greatly underestimated. Hilton (1993) notes that one industry executive in 1916 said that "the fad feature of automobile riding will gradually wear off" (p. 51). This is the archetypical symptom of the silent war situation: a known alternative is discounted. The interurbans tried to compete with automobiles by hauling freight but they were soon overwhelmed as trucks grew in use. To a great extent, the railroads continue to face this competition today.

This brief chronicle of the railroad industry offers a compelling elaboration of the pattern of situations leading to consolidation.

After a long gestation period (evolution), technology matures (crossing the chasm), and explosive market growth ensues (steady growth). Numerous players enter the market and prices plummet as they scramble to gain or maintain a share of the market. This competition leads to financial woes, which result in many failures and mergers (consolidation) and, consequently, a dramatic decrease in the number of players. For companies facing such transitions, it is essential to be able to assess the likely course of consolidation, as well as the company's likely role—that is, acquirer or acquired—in this situation. With this understanding, they can take advantage of opportunities and avert crises.

The Automobile Industry

The notion of a self-powered passenger vehicle dates far back in time. Early experiments include those of Leonardo da Vinci and Robert Valturio, who planned for a wind carriage in 1472. Two-masted wind carriages were invented in the Netherlands in 1600. Belgian priest Ferdinand Verbeist created a steam-propelled carriage in China in 1678. Jacques de Vaucanson developed a carriage propelled by a large clockwork in 1748. A gas-powered vehicle was demonstrated in Paris by Isaac de Rivas in 1807.

However, the first true automobile was designed by another Frenchman, Nicolas-Joseph Cugnot, in 1769. This automobile was a steam-powered tricycle and was capable of maintaining 2.25 miles per hour for twenty minutes. Germans Carl Benz and Gottlieb Daimler are credited with the first gasoline-engine automobile in 1885. The Daimler-Benz automobile company was founded in 1895.

In the United States, George Selden filed a patent for the automobile in 1879. Charles and Frank Duryea created an American gas-powered automobile in 1892–93. The first commercially successful American-made automobile was the three-horsepower Oldsmobile in 1901, named after automobile industry pioneer Ransom Eli Olds.

By 1898, there were 50 automobile companies in the United States. Between 1904 and 1908, 241 automobile companies went into business. Thus, the familiar pattern recurred: a technology matured over a long period of time, and then rather suddenly, after successful commercialization of the technology, hundreds of companies formed in hopes of making their fortunes with it. The automobile industry was in a steady growth situation, but the stage was already set for consolidation.

Interestingly, competition between variations in the technology itself was not fully resolved at the turn of the century. At that point, 40 percent of U.S. automobiles were powered by steam, 38 percent by electricity, and 22 percent by gasoline. Also of interest, the automobile was not an instant success in the mass market. Henry Ford produced eight versions of his cars—models A, B, C, F, K, N, R, and S—before gaining success with the Model T in 1908. With the Model T, the mass market could now afford to own an automobile. The chasm was crossed.

James Womack, Daniel Jones, and Daniel Roos chronicle the subsequent development of the automobile industry in *The Machine That Changed the World* (1991). They emphasize that Ford's success in producing a car for "everyman" was the result of his transformation of manufacturing from centuries of craft production into the age of mass production. Forty years later, Eiji Toyoda and Taiichi Ohno in Japan transformed mass production into lean production; we will return to this story a bit later.

The problem with craft production, despite its appealing image of hand-crafted quality products, is that it costs too much, far too much for most people to afford. Through extreme specialization in manufacturing techniques, Ford was able to reduce costs substantially and thereby enable mass markets.

Craft production is characterized by a highly skilled workforce, extreme decentralization, general-purpose tools, and low production volumes. Because no company can exercise a monopoly over these types of resources, it was easy to enter the automobile business when it was in this early stage of production. By 1905, hundreds of companies in Western Europe and North America were producing small volumes of autos using craft techniques. The high costs of this method of production naturally resulted in high prices and an automobile market that was limited to the upper middle class and higher.

To lower prices so that a mass market would be possible, the costs of production had to be lowered. Ford's innovation of mass production focused on the complete and consistent interchangeability of parts and simplicity in attaching them to one another. Interchangeability, simplicity, and ease of attachment enabled Ford to eliminate skilled fitters, the people who crafted each individual car together by forming, filing, and otherwise manipulating idiosyncratic components.

The impact of this innovation can be measured in terms of the average cycle time, that is, the average time before each individual operation was repeated by a production worker. Before Ford's innovation, the average cycle time was 514 minutes. With interchangeability, simplicity, and ease of attachment, the average cycle time was reduced to 2.3 minutes. In 1913, Ford added continuous flow assembly lines, and the average decreased to 1.2 minutes.

Ford also perfected the interchangeability of workers. Mass production jobs were so simplified that they required only a few minutes of training. Consequently, untrained and unskilled workers could easily fill the jobs. Of course, industrial engineers had to think through how all the parts would come together and just what each assembler would do. In this way, the engineers became the knowledge workers, taking over the role formerly played by the machine shop owners and factory foremen of the earlier craft era.

An important result of Ford's mass production technique was extreme centralization of control. But his penchant for this type of control, centralized in himself, became a limiting factor in the growth of his company. John Staudenmaier in "Henry Ford's Big Flaw" (Invention & Technology, 1994), discusses the ways in which Ford's obsession with control tended to suffocate the successful company he had created. Fortunately, as is typical, the growth of this thriving industry did not depend on one person.

Alfred Sloan provided the next innovation. Sloan was hired by William Durant, the founder of General Motors, to straighten out the enterprise that had been created by his acquisition of several car manufacturing companies. Sloan added professional management to Ford's basic concept of mass production. Professional financial and marketing specialists were added to the engineering specialists created by Ford. Sloan also standardized the internal systems and components of cars, further lowering costs. The overall result for the industry was a revolution in marketing and management.

Ford lured people into the routine and boring jobs of mass production with high wages, the infamous $5 per day. The nature of these jobs caused people to focus on work conditions, including seniority and job rights, in the face of cyclical auto markets. As a result, they borrowed an innovation from the railroads, job control unionism. The combination of Ford's factory practices, Sloan's marketing and management techniques, and organized labor's control of job assignments and work tasks resulted in the final maturation of mass production.

Womack, Jones, and Roos (1991) use this understanding of the emergence and maturation of mass production as a backdrop upon which to describe Japan's innovations in lean production. They emphasize the Japanese culture's inability to adapt to mass production. Japanese requirements for lifetime employment made impossible the large hirings and layoffs typical in industries characterized by mass production. Since people were employed for life, it only made sense to invest in them so that they had multiple skills that would benefit the company.

With this point of view in mind, Taiichi Ohno's pioneering work at Toyota led to the paradigm of lean production. Ohno began by experimenting with flat team concepts. He also reconsidered the supplier-assembler relationship and decided that the goals of low cost and high quality could best be achieved through a close working relationship and long-term commitment. He developed a new way to coordinate the flow of parts within the supply system on a day-to-day basis, which is called the just-in-time system or *kanban* at Toyota. The principles of lean production were fully worked out by the 1960s, but it wasn't until the 1980s that the world arrived at the same point in the diffusion of lean production that it had achieved in the 1920s with mass production.

Several key organizational features are central to lean production. Design and development occur in parallel and are team-oriented in terms of communication, authority, and rewards. As far as production is concerned, the maximum number of tasks and responsibilities are transferred to the production workers actually adding value to the car on the line. Doing this requires giving them far more professional skills than in mass production. These skills are applied creatively in this team setting rather than in a rigid hierarchy.

Another central characteristic is incorporation of a system for detecting defects in a way that quickly traces every problem to its ultimate cause. This system, in addition to the team orientation, results in the much-heralded continuous quality improvement programs of Japanese car manufacturers. The penchant for quality in particular and lean production in general has slowly but surely reached non-Japanese car manufacturers. For example, Ford worked with Mazda, Rover worked with Honda. Interestingly, both of these efforts were prompted by the crises that are often precursors of major change.

Womack, Jones, and Roos (1991) visited many plants around the world to assess the extent to which lean production has been adopted. They note that many plants in the United States have attempted to use high technology to eliminate production workers. However, they conclude that without an appropriate organization, the high-tech solution can result in adding many indirect technical and service workers, undermining any potential gains in productivity. Their visits to European auto factories sometimes led to the conclusion that the culture was still at the craft stage even though it was trying mass production and aspiring to lean production.

The authors conclude their chronicle of the automobile industry by noting that Ford and Sloan built upon earlier production and management innovations in the railroad and other industries.

Although they did not originate the elements of their systems, they were, nevertheless, the first to create such comprehensive systems.

By 1920, mass production was broadly embraced in the United States. The result was a crossover situation in these companies, which enabled transitions to study growth situations. Europe, in contrast, abandoned craft production only very reluctantly. The Europeans waited until after World War II, when guest workers became available who were willing to tolerate the working conditions mass production required. Postwar Japan provided an opportunity, and perhaps a necessity, for rethinking automobile production. This situation precipitated a creative environment for Taiichi Ohno as well as fertile ground for the concepts of thinkers such as W. Edwards Deming. As a result, the emerging dominant paradigm in the automobile industry is lean production, which Womack and his colleagues argue is to everybody's benefit.

Reflecting on this brief history of the automobile industry, a few patterns may be discerned. First, we see yet again versions of the consolidation situation. Whereas there were hundreds of automobile companies in the United States in the early 1900s, there are now three. Some of the U.S. automobile market has been lost to offshore producers, but the total number of car companies is still small, about twenty or so. Thus, roughly 1 percent of those originally in existence have survived in some form or another.

We also see examples of the silent war situation. In fact, Magaziner and Patinkin (1989) see the Japanese auto industry as an example of a competitor going unacknowledged until it is almost too late.

This chronicle also illustrates the process situation, which involves taking existing product innovations and adding value in terms of process innovations (see Chapter Two for a more detailed discussion). The result is higher-quality, lower-cost versions of products. Although the original product innovations are likely to have created demand for these products—in other words, created the market—process innovations may take over the market. Thus, originators of product concepts do not necessarily survive to reap the benefits of mass markets. Henry Ford and Alfred Sloan proved this and so did Taiichi Ohno.

The history of the automobile industry also provides examples of the crossover situation, where one industry innovates through wholesale adoption of another industry's technologies and practices. (Again, see Chapter Two for more discussion.) We saw this with Ford and Sloan's adoption of the practices pioneered in the railroad industry and elsewhere.

Another interesting example of the crossover situation occurred with the invention of the military tank. Niles White describes this process in "From Tractor to Tank" (*Invention & Technology*, 1993). Benjamin Holt created the first steam traction engine—a tractor—in 1890. Faced with the problem of plowing marshland, he added tracks, a centuries-old idea, in 1904. He called the resulting vehicle the *Caterpillar*, which became his company's trademark in 1910. By 1916, Holt had sold two thousand machines in more than twenty countries. Thus, it took over twenty years from Holt's initial tractor until substantial business success. This is a good example of the evolution situation.

The British army, in the person of Ernest Swindon, approached Holt with the idea of creating a tracked military vehicle, the tank. Holt was not interested in military applications. However, this did not deter Swindon. He subsequently wrote Holt to thank him for proving that the technology would work so that the British army could proceed with confidence. Thus, the tracked vehicle concept crossed over from one industry to another.

In my work with companies in the automobile industry, I have been struck with how very similar cars are. Most, if not all, innovations are relatively small and are diffused throughout the industry quickly. This situation has many of the characteristics of commodity trap situations. As a consequence, great emphasis is placed on quality control and cost control as well as on marketing and sales. Margins are inherently low and profits come with high sales volumes.

Why would anyone want to be in such a business? The primary answer is probably that they are already in the business. They have made major capital investments and they have to take advantage of these commitments. In other words, they may be organically unable to make substantial changes. (This kind of limitation is discussed in great detail in Chapter Seven in the context of the defense industry.)

One strategy for extricating a company from such a situation is to pursue multiple situations simultaneously. For example, a company may have no choice but to pursue a process situation for its traditional, mainstream business, but vision quest, evolution, and crossover situations can be pursued in parallel (see Chapter Four for more on this). With patience and persistence, one or more of these situations may lead to robust steady growth situations in three to five years.

The Aircraft Industry

People have always been fascinated with the idea of flight. Serious speculation about flight occupied such thinkers as Roger Bacon in the thirteenth century and Leonardo da Vinci in the fifteenth century. In the seventeenth century John Wilkins forecast the evolution of fixed-wing aircraft. During the eighteenth and nineteenth centuries, science fiction writers, including Jules Verne in France, popularized the idea of flight.

Frenchman Felix du Temple attempted but failed to demonstrate full-scale powered flight in 1857. Samuel Pierpont Langley demonstrated in 1901 the first flight of a heavier-than-air vehicle powered by a gasoline engine. In that year, he also tried two tests on a manned vehicle but both ended in failure. However, Langley's aircraft was later (in 1914) reconditioned by Glenn Curtiss and, with a few modifications, flown for brief periods.

In December 1903, Orville Wright flew for twelve seconds and landed without damage. On his fourth flight the next day, Wilbur Wright flew for fifty-nine seconds, covering 852 feet. The aviation era was not yet born, however. Orville and Wilbur had much marketing and sales ahead of them. Finally, in 1908 they secured a government contract to build and deliver an aircraft for $25,000.

Thus, as with the three previous industries we have looked at in this chapter—steamboats, railroads, and automobiles—there was a long gestation period in the development of aircraft technology. The aviation industry then matured quite slowly because of the capital and risks involved. Government support was needed, usually in the form of military procurements or mail delivery contracts. The government faced the choice of providing this contract support to aviation or establishing outright public ownership of the industry to ensure its survival.

The government's role broadened with the formation of the National Advisory Committee for Aeronautics (NACA) in 1915, which later became the National Aeronautics and Space Administration (NASA). It was authorized to own laboratories and perform research. The first facility was Langley Field in Virginia.

John B. Rae chronicles the development of the aviation industry in *Climb to Greatness* (1968). The story began as the seeds of World War I were being sown. In 1914 the Census Bureau located 16 aircraft manufacturers with a combined total output for the year of 49 planes. By 1918, the American aircraft industry was delivering 14,000 aircraft and employed 175,000 people. However, with the signing of the World War I armistice, one hundred million dollars in contracts were canceled in just a few days. Production dropped from 14,000 in 1918 to 263 in 1922.

The strongest surviving companies included the Curtiss Aeroplane Company, Boeing Airplane Company, and Wright Aeronautical Company. The founder of the Curtiss Company was Glenn Curtiss. The Boeing Company was founded by William Boeing, who had made his first fortune in the lumber business. The Wright Aeronautical Company was the Wright-Martin Company until Glen Martin left in 1917. Wright-Martin emerged from the sale of the Wright Company (formed by the Wright brothers) to Martin in 1915.

Several aircraft companies were founded in the 1920s. Douglas Aircraft was formed by Donald Douglas, a former chief engineer for Glenn Martin. Sikorsky Aero Engineering Corporation was founded by Igor Sikorsky. Pratt & Whitney was formed by Frederick Rentschler. Lockheed was founded by the Loughead brothers. Other new companies included Detroit Aircraft (which eventually owned 87 percent of Lockheed), Grumman Aircraft, Aviation Corporation (AVCO), Fairchild Engine and Airplane Company, and Ryan Aeronautical Company.

In 1925, California was home to four aircraft companies and New York to fifteen. Then, in 1927 Charles Lindbergh's solo flight across the Atlantic sold the American people on commercial aviation. The chasm was crossed. There were three hundred aircraft factories by 1928.

Thus, the aircraft industry was booming, at least in terms of new companies if not profits. Many of the company names we now view as synonymous with aviation were in business during this steady growth situation. Many others, which few of us recall, were formed but then disappeared.

With the increasing maturity of the industry, aircraft manufacturers began to think in terms of vertical integration, including operating their own airlines and building their own airframes, engines, and components. For example, Boeing reorganized as the United Aircraft and Transportation Company in 1929. With such developments, the possibility emerged for a few large companies to dominate the industry.

The Air Mail Act of 1934 ended this possibility. In compliance with this legislation, United separated into three segments. Boeing again became the Boeing Airplane Company. The airline subsidiaries became United Airlines. The eastern manufacturing divisions—Pratt and Whitney, Hamilton Standard, Chance Vought, and Sikorsky—became the United Aircraft Corporation.

North American and AVCO followed the same general pattern. North American was reconstituted as a manufacturing concern and its airlines organized into two companies, Transcontinental and Western (TWA) and Eastern. AVCO's aircraft manufacturing divisions became the Aviation Manufacturing Corporation and its transport company emerged as American Airlines.

In the 1930s, commercial aviation was dominated by Douglas Aircraft's DC-3. Within two years of its introduction, Douglas had sold more than eight hundred of them and they were carrying 95 percent of the nation's civil air traffic. Only about a dozen companies competed in military aircraft. Four airframe manufacturers (Douglas, Boeing, Curtiss-Wright, and North American) and two engine manufacturers (Curtiss-Wright and Pratt & Whitney) dominated.

However, there were still new entries, in part as a result of quickly changing technologies for airframes, wings, propellers, and landing gear. When United Aircraft and Transport decided to move its Avion subsidiary (founded by John K. Northrop) to Wichita, Northrop left United to form Northrop Corporation because he wanted to stay in Los Angeles. Douglas Aircraft owned half the stock of this new company. Other companies formed in this period included the Seversky Aircraft Corporation (later Republic Aviation Corporation), Beech Aircraft Corporation, Bell Aircraft Corporation, Piper Aircraft Corporation, and McDonnell Aircraft Corporation. Consolidated Aircraft in San Diego became Convair.

Despite the growth in the number of players in the industry, all were still dependent on government orders to avoid crises. Not until the closing days of the 1930s, with a new war looming, were even the major firms secure. With the onset of World War II, aircraft production soared. But by the end of 1945 contracts valued at over $21 billion were canceled, and only sixteen aircraft plants remained in operation out of the sixty-six that had been functioning a year earlier.

Four of the five large West Coast companies—Boeing, Douglas, Lockheed, and North American—emerged from the war in reasonably strong positions. In contrast, Convair was not in good shape. Although the prices of aircraft had increased substantially over a fifteen-year period—rising from $50,000 for the Boeing 247 to $1,250,000 for the Boeing 377—aircraft companies were still losing money.

The Finletter Commission in 1947 analyzed the problems of the aircraft industry and concluded, among other things, that government-dominated demand, which fluctuated violently and caused a lack of production continuity, undermined efforts to maintain a workforce. The commission also noted that the industry was characterized by high engineering costs, extremely long manufacturing cycles, and rapid obsolescence.

By 1949 six West Coast airframe companies—Boeing, Convair, Douglas, Lockheed, North American, and Northrop—had 69 percent of the total dollar value of military orders. Only two newcomers—McDonnell and Beech—were among the top sixteen aircraft manufacturers. Thus, consolidation continued unabated, as it has to this day. For example, thus far in the 1990s, Lockheed has bought General Dynamics' aircraft operations, Northrop has bought Grumman, and most recently Lockheed and Martin-Marietta have merged.

In 1949, Glenn Martin, a great pioneer in aviation, left the Martin Company. By 1953, the Martin Company was effectively out of the airframe business. In 1954, Chance Vought was separated from United Aircraft. Later in the 1950s, General Dynamics bought Convair.

As late as 1958, over half of the commercial aircraft in the world were built by Douglas, which had continually built on the success of the DC-3. However, Boeing quickly moved into jet aircraft, mostly as a result of military contracts. Using the military KC-135 as a starting point, Boeing introduced the 707 commercial transport in 1958. Douglas was much slower to shift paradigms. The DC-8 did not appear until 1959. Boeing's early gamble on jet aircraft provided the basis for its strong position in commercial aviation today. Douglas has yet to fully recover from the experience of this paradigm lost situation.

The 1960s saw many mergers and continued consolidation. Textron acquired the Bell Aerospace Corporation. Vought and its Dallas neighbors merged to form Ling-Temco-Vought in 1961. Temco (Texas Engineering and Manufacturing Company) had been founded in 1945. Also in 1961, the Martin Company expanded beyond the aerospace field by merging with the Marietta Corporation, a manufacturer of cement, lime, and rock products as well as chemicals. The resulting company became the Martin-Marietta Corporation, which in the 1990s acquired several military electronics firms and then, as noted earlier, merged with Lockheed.

In 1967, North American merged with Rockwell-Standard to become North American Rockwell Corporation. Also in 1967, Douglas merged with McDonnell to become McDonnell-Douglas Corporation. Such consolidation became necessary so that the resulting few large concerns could withstand the feast-and-famine cycle typical of the industry. By the 1990s, three airframe manufacturers controlled the commercial aircraft industry, including a dominant Boeing, a heavily subsidized Airbus, and a very much weakened Douglas. Similarly, a few avionics companies dominated, as did three aircraft engine companies. Today, consolidation seems nearly complete.

In addition to the compelling example of consolidation that this chronicle of the aircraft industry offers, several other situations characterize the industry. T. A. Heppenheimer in "The Dream of the Flying Wing" (*Invention & Technology*, 1994) tells of John K. Northrop's fascination with the possibility of a flying wing. Unlike a typical aircraft, whose wings are attached to its fuselage, a flying wing is an aircraft that is basically all wing.

Jack Northrop was born in 1895. By the time he was twenty years old, he was a regular visitor at the auto and airplane shop of Allan and Malcolm Loughhead. Northrop's first aircraft design was the Loughhead S-1. Unfortunately, in the postwar economy there were few contracts and Loughhead folded in 1920.

Northrop joined Donald Douglas in 1923. Working in his spare time, Northrop developed what was to become the Vega. He went to work for a rejuvenated Loughhead—now Lockheed—in 1926, and the first Vega emerged in 1927. It was a big hit and provided Northrop with a little freedom to focus on the flying wing.

Although the concept of a flying wing was not new, no one had ever actually built one. Allan Loughhead would not back Northrop, so he started a new company, the Avion Corporation, with the backing of the Hearst publishing family. A demonstration flight was held in 1930.

Then the Depression hit. Boeing bought out Avion in 1931 and decided to move this operation to Wichita, Kansas. But Northrop did not want to move to the Midwest. He left to join Douglas in a joint venture and participated in the development of the DC-2 and DC-3. Douglas bought him out in 1937. The proceeds of this deal led to the creation of the Northrop Corporation in which, as noted earlier, Douglas was a shareholder.

Northrop's next flying wing took to the air in 1940–1941. He subsequently won a contract during World War II to build a bomber using this concept, the B-35, which was given a flight test in 1946. His competition, the B-36, was canceled in 1948. Meanwhile, Northrop won a contract to build thirty B-49s, a jet-powered version of the B-35. However, contract negotiations broke down when he would not agree to build the B-49 in Texas, and consequently the B-36 was resuscitated.

Efforts to save the B-49 floundered on technical arguments. The flying wing, it was argued, was too heavy and created too much drag at high speeds. In late 1949, the order came to scrap the eleven existing B-49s. Soon after, Northrop got a contract to produce the F-89 fighter but, according to Heppenheimer, he was nevertheless crushed and never got over it.

The story ends in 1980. Northrop, now old and feeble in a wheelchair, saw the blueprints for the B-2 stealth bomber. The stealth properties of the flying wing, which Northrop had not foreseen, had vindicated his vision. Of particular pertinence to the discussion of this chapter, it had taken over fifty years for his vision to be realized.

Curt Wohleber tells a similar story in "Straight Up" (*Invention & Technology*, 1993), the story of Igor Sikorsky's vision of the helicopter. Sikorsky built his first prototype helicopters in 1909 and 1910 while he was still in Russia. He then shifted his attention to fixed-wing aircraft, first in Russia and subsequently in the United States where, as noted earlier, he formed Sikorsky Aero Engineering Corporation. His company later became a division of United Aircraft.

In 1938, Sikorsky proposed to United Aircraft that a helicopter be built. The first test flight of his VS-300 occurred in September 1939 when Sikorsky was fifty. (VS stood for Vought-Sikorsky as a result of the merger of United Aircraft's Sikorsky and Chance Vought divisions.) Although the VS-300 was very good at hovering, unfortunately it was not good at forward motion, especially straight forward motion.

His next helicopter was the XR-4, which was a military prototype. By the end of World War II, four hundred R-4, R-5, and R-6 helicopters had been produced. However, commercial use was slow to gain favor and it took quite a few years before helicopters were commonly used for other than military purposes. It took over thirty years for Sikorsky to realize his vision and over forty until this vision resulted in business success.

The stories of Jack Northrop and Igor Sikorsky are similar in that it took several decades for their visions to be realized. This certainly qualifies them as examples of evolution situations. In particular, these stories epitomize the slow maturation of technology from initial vision to commercial viability.

The Northrop and Sikorsky stories also provide examples of vision quest situations. This type of situation involves an individual, or occasionally a team, persisting over a very long period of time to make a dream come true. (Chapter Two discusses this in more detail.) Often the individuals are way ahead of their times; the technologies necessary to realize their dreams may not yet even be available. This may deter them for a time, but they eventually return to pursue their dreams. Many if not most dreams are never fulfilled. However, this possibility does not often occur to those on vision quests.

The aviation industry also provides examples of silent war situations. One of these is chronicled by T. A. Heppenheimer in "The Jet Plane Is Born" (*Invention & Technology*, 1993). Going into World War II, other countries could not compete with U.S. aircraft engine technology. America's piston-driven airplanes were far superior because of the turbocharger, which enabled American planes to achieve unprecedented altitude and speed. Rather than attempt to catch up, the English and Germans turned their attention to the unproven idea of jets. The Americans, smug in their advantage, discounted the jet engine's potential. Thus, a big advantage almost became a very big disadvantage, and the United States was nearly left behind. Collaboration with the British during World War II fortunately enabled this country to catch up.

This brief vignette epitomizes the silent war situation: the victim of the competition does not even realize that competition is happening. It may be aware of the competing technology but completely discounts its potential. Thus, the company sits by and unknowingly provides few if any barriers to the success of its competitors.

A contemporary version of the silent war situation involves Airbus, the government-sponsored European consortium of English, French, German, and Spanish aircraft companies. Airbus has succeeded in becoming second in the commercial aircraft market, displacing McDonnell-Douglas, which is now a distant third. But Boeing and Douglas are very much aware of this competition and are trying to preempt it.

However, U.S. companies face a disadvantage: the U.S. government is not willing to provide the support that European governments do. Although the U.S. government provides military development contracts and aviation R&D funding through agencies like NASA, it does not involve itself directly with issues such as financing airline purchases of U.S.-built commercial aircraft. Thus, a silent war is going on because the potential victim (the United States) has apparently discounted the impact of one or more key competitive advantages of the adversary.

I have been involved with the aviation industry for more than twenty-five years, at first in R&D and more recently on the business side. I have chaired a couple of long-range planning committees that focused on technology trends and potential operational problems. I have also conducted numerous planning workshops and projects for aircraft and avionics companies. Recently, I served on an advisory committee for Boeing that focused on evaluating the cockpit design for the new Boeing 777 aircraft. As a result of my experiences, I see the following prospects for the industry.

As is readily apparent from this historical account, the aircraft industry has gone through a tremendous amount of consolidation. There are only a handful of players, and they all know each other very well. Substantial effort is invested in trying to differentiate their offerings in terms of performance, economy, and safety.

However, the industry faces a dilemma characterized by the saying, "You spend money in the cockpit, save money in maintenance, and make money in the cabin." In other words, the firms in the industry spend money to assure performance, economy, and safety and try to meet all maintenance requirements as economically as possible. However, they make money only by satisfying passengers.

From the passenger's perspective, all airplanes are pretty much the same. What matters is comfort, service, and price. Furthermore, business passengers, who provide most of the profits, increasingly want "office-in-the sky" capabilities such as telephone, fax, and computer. An awareness of this trend led me to suggest, during one of my planning workshops with an aircraft company, that the winners in the airline competition would be those who provide the best information technology to passengers. The aircraft itself would become, in effect, a computer cabinet and not the essence of the value in the industry.

This may seem an outlandish idea, but it was taken very seriously. The aircraft could become, in effect, a commodity much as automobiles have. The profit margins would then be greatest for those providing the information technology. For aircraft manufacturers, a dearly held paradigm would then be lost. They would find themselves in a commodity trap situation.

This scenario is already beginning to emerge. The organic nature of aircraft companies and their huge capital investments may necessitate that they simply accept this fate. In fact, this possibility was recently acknowledged by a Boeing executive in the industry magazine *Interavia* (Wilson, 1994). If aircraft companies take such scenarios seriously, they may be able avoid many of the snares of the commodity trap.

Summary

The histories of the steamboat, railroad, automobile, and aircraft industries can greatly enrich our understanding of the ten common situations introduced in Chapter Two. Each of these industries provides examples of the evolution situation as the technologies underlying them all took very long times to mature—as many as one hundred to two hundred years.

Nevertheless, these technologies were viewed as revolutionary at the time of their relatively sudden market success. Similarly, we now see information technologies as revolutionary. But the revolution really has come in their impact on our lives rather than in the emergence of the technologies. This chapter has also shown that every era has its high-tech trends and events. We are not unique in being challenged by these types of changes.

It is easy to imagine the atmosphere surrounding the development of steamboats in the early 1800s, railroads in the mid 1800s, automobiles at the turn of the century, and aircraft in the early 1900s. I am sure that the pioneers and entrepreneurs in these industries keenly felt the exhilaration of change and competition. Their stories of change affected them as substantially as stories today affect us.

The chronicles of this chapter also offer numerous examples of the silent war situation: the impact of the railroads on stagecoaches and canal boats, of automobiles on railroads and particularly on the interurbans, of the Japanese automobile manufacturers' innovations on U.S. and European manufacturers, of the English and German jet engines on U.S. piston engine manufacturers, and of government-sponsored Airbus on Boeing and Douglas. In all of these examples, industry leaders calmly enjoyed their position while often-acknowledged but usually discounted competitors took away their markets.

The chronicles of this chapter also provided many examples of the consolidation situation. Opportunity emerges and companies proliferate. Overexpansion results in price cutting to gain market share. Profits disappear. The industry consolidates to just a few dominant players who mature and often become institutionalized. This situation has been dramatically played out in all the industries discussed in this chapter.

There were also examples of the process and crossover situations. Ford and Sloan innovated in terms of process changes in the automobile industry, as did Ohno more recently. Crossover involves seeing connections rather than creating technologies. The crossover situation occurred when Ford and Sloan borrowed many of their innovations from the railroad industry and elsewhere and when the military adopted the tracked vehicle concept from the farm machinery and heavy equipment industry.

Finally, there were several examples of the vision quest. Northrop's vision of the flying wing and Sikorsky's vision of the helicopter are primary examples; Ford's vision of a mass market for automobiles is another. Holt's vision of tracked vehicles is yet another illustration.

The vision quest illustrates the effects that men and women can have on their times, in contrast to the effects that their times have on them. The vision quest proceeds even when the times are not ready. Patience, persistence, and often passion drive people to overcome obstacles and eventually succeed. While this situation seems quite positive, perhaps even uplifting, it also has drawbacks, not the least of which may be decades of business failure until success eventually emerges.

Finally, let's review the distinction between organic and synthetic perspectives in anticipating, recognizing, and responding to change. The chronicles of this chapter illustrated many attempts to synthesize new organizations in response to the organic processes of consolidation. However, because the chapter focused on industry segments as wholes rather than on individual companies, it is difficult to comprehend how the enterprises involved attempted to balance organic and synthetic perspectives. In Chapters Six and Seven greater emphasis is placed on individual enterprises. This tightened focus will enable exploration of the more detailed processes of change.

6

Computers

Creating a New Market

Computers have become increasingly pervasive in the past decade. Computers are central to many jobs, including bank teller, passenger reservation agent, supervisor of manufacturing robots, and business executive. Many people also have computers in their homes.

In 1983, *Time* magazine heralded the ubiquity of the computer by bestowing the prestige of its yearly award and accompanying cover story to a computer rather than to a person (Rosenblatt, 1983). Does this mean that the computer revolution has finally occurred? I think the answer is no. Rather, computers have sufficiently matured that the majority of us accept them as everyday technology.

Computer technology and the computer industry evolved over hundreds of years. Although names such as Bill Gates or Steve Jobs may seem to be synonymous with computing, these luminaries are only the most recent entrepreneurs to wave the computing banner. This chapter discusses a long series of entrepreneurs and business leaders who led their enterprises through periods of dramatic transitions, occasionally with success and more often with substantial stumbles.

It is important to differentiate computing technology from the computer industry. Computing technology is very old, dating from the abacus that was invented thousands of years ago. People have had reason to add and subtract numbers for a long, long time.

The first mechanical adding machine was built more than three hundred years ago by Frenchman Blaise Pascal. German Gottfried

Wilhelm Liebniz, after seeing Pascal's machine, created the Stepped Reckoner in 1673. This device could also multiply, divide, and perform square roots. The first commercially available calculator was Thomas de Colmar's arithmometer, invented in 1820.

Charles Babbage conceived of the first digital computer in the 1830s. He envisioned it—the Analytical Engine—as powered by steam. (As discussed in Chapter Five, steam power was high technology in the 1830s.) However, Babbage's vision was never realized because there were no precision techniques for fabricating parts.

Babbage got his idea for a digital computer from Frenchman Joseph-Marie Jacquard's punch-card programmed looms, which were developed in the early 1800s. He was also aware of the work of Englishman George Boole, who performed pioneering research in binary logic in the mid 1800s. Binary logic later became key to electronic computing.

Jacquard's punched card method for controlling looms also influenced American Herman Hollerith, who invented a card-based system for tabulating the results of the 1890 census. Hollerith's venture led to what would later become International Business Machines (IBM) under the leadership of Thomas J. Watson, Sr. In *Father, Son, and Co.* (1990), Thomas J. Watson, Jr. not surprisingly asserts that, "In the history of industrialization, punch-card machines belong right up there with the Jacquard loom, the cotton gin, and the locomotive" (p. 73). The adoption of punched cards for computing constitutes a good example of a crossover situation.

With the mention of IBM, we now shift the emphasis from computing technology to the computing industry. The many stories underlying the evolution of this industry provide a rich array of insights into how enterprises deal with change. Many of these stories begin in the mid 1800s.

Roots of the Industry

James W. Cortada in *Before the Computer* (1993) chronicles the emergence of the computer industry in the period between 1865 and 1956. During this time, IBM, National Cash Register Company (NCR), Burroughs, Remington-Rand, and other companies became dominant in the business equipment industry with tabulators (IBM), cash registers (NCR), calculators (Burroughs), and typewriters (Remington). Their dominance in these industries set the stage for their primacy in the computer market.

Cortada notes that many mechanical aids were available for computing and managing data long before computers became available. William S. Burroughs saw the market need for adding machines. James Ritty and later John H. Patterson envisioned the potential demand for cash registers. Christopher L. Sholes identified the potential for typewriters. As already noted, Herman Hollerith invented a tabulator to compile the results of the U.S. census. Before 1920, these business machines were all independently sold with each individual company offering only one type of machine. Subsequently, these companies expanded into all of the different machines.

It is interesting to think about the reasons for the demand for these business machines. Cortada (1993) argues that starting in the 1840s the American economy went through a long period—more than a hundred years—of continual expansion and industrialization. Despite the Civil War in the 1860s, the financial panic in the 1870s, and a severe depression in the 1890s, the economic expansion continued with major new ventures in railroads, steel mills, and chemical plants. This expansion required more than substantial investment in technology alone. Investments in marketing and distribution channels and the development of management systems were also central to success. These kinds of investments provided the impetus for the development of the business machines discussed in the following paragraphs.

As noted earlier, adding machines and calculators date back hundreds of years to mathematicians like Pascal and Liebniz who sought aids to calculation. After several years of work, William Burroughs patented an adding machine in 1885, the same year that he formed the Arithmometer Company. Burroughs was not the only one to sense the potential market for calculators. For example, Dorr E. Felt invented one of the first key-operated calculating machines and the firm of Felt and Tarrant was formed in 1886.

By 1895, following fifteen years of work by Burroughs, the calculator market started to blossom. By the time of Burroughs' death in 1898 his company's products had achieved some market acceptance. The Burroughs adding and listing machine was quite popular by the early 1900s. In recognition of his contributions, the company was reincorporated in 1904 as the Burroughs Adding Machine Company. Thus, almost twenty-five years after he started the company and eight years after his death, Burroughs was an unqualified success in another example of both vision quest and evolution situations. My guess is that Burroughs, like most entrepreneurs, never thought success would come so slowly.

However, this slowly emerging victory was not complete and, in retrospect, was temporary. There was a crowded field of competitors in the calculator business. Frequently emerging technological improvements had to be matched, or even established vendors could be superseded by other, typically newer, firms. These firms usually had a single product or technology to sell. Interestingly, if we change the word "calculator" to "software," this paragraph would describe a modern industry as aptly as it does one that existed almost a hundred years ago.

The cash register was invented by James Ritty in the late 1870s in Dayton, Ohio. A few years later, Ritty sold the business to Jacob Eckert, who renamed the company the National Manufacturing Company. John Patterson bought a controlling interest in 1884 and changed the company's name to National Cash Register Company. By 1888, Patterson had a payroll of eighty.

Patterson is remembered as the entrepreneur who made salesmanship into a science; his disciples included Thomas J. Watson, Sr. John Patterson thoroughly trained his salespeople and continually refined the marketing and sales approach that enabled selling cash registers. Nevertheless, by 1895, eighty-four companies were selling or attempting to sell cash registers. Considering the indicators in

Exhibit 4.2, it is clear that the cash register industry was in the early stages of a consolidation situation.

Although, once again, early developments in typewriter technology dated back over 150 years, this machine too emerged during this period. It was Christopher Sholes who developed the typewriter to the point of being marketable, obtaining financial backing from James Densmore, who found an established manufacturing company, Remington, to manufacture it.

Remington had significant difficulties gaining momentum because of marketing problems, which is often the case for start-ups. In addition, competitors emerged quickly in the typewriter market. Remington was also slow to respond to technological change, which affected its sales. These problems and others continued to plague Remington throughout the emergence of the computer industry and, as later discussed, led to the loss of its decisive lead in the computer industry in the 1950s.

By the early 1900s, there were four large typewriter companies, including the former Remington (now called the Union Typewriter Company), Underwood, L. C. Smith, and Royal. At this point, the industry exhibited elements of a crossing the chasm situation as well as elements of an early consolidation situation. Thus, the problems that the computer hardware industry faced in the late 1980s and early 1990s and the problems that are now likely to emerge in the computer software industry are by no means unusual in the business machines industries.

Herman Hollerith developed the concept for the tabulator while he was working as a clerk at the Census Bureau. Cortada notes that Hollerith's idea was at least in part the result of comments made by John S. Billings, director of the Division of Vital Statistics, that "there ought to be some mechanical way of doing this job, something on the principle of the Jacquard loom" (1993, p. 46).

Hollerith was at the center of the resulting tabulating technology for many years. He single-handedly formed the Tabulating Machine Company in 1889, and his tabulating equipment was used for the census of 1890. Hollerith joined others to form the

Computing-Tabulating-Recording Company (C-T-R) in 1911 because he needed an infusion of capital to continue expanding. Thomas J. Watson, Sr., a former NCR executive, was hired in 1914 as general manager. The company changed its name to IBM in 1924.

One of Hollerith's contributions to the industry was his pioneering practice of renting data processing equipment. Under Watson's tutelage, constant introduction of new products led to continual success. These product innovations came for the most part in response to customer demands and careful monitoring of competitive offerings.

The Census Bureau decided that it needed more than a single source of tabulating equipment. To this end, it encouraged James Powers, another employee, to create competing equipment. Powers left the Census Bureau in 1911 to form the Powers Accounting Machine Company. The U.S. government gave Powers the right to patent the devices he had developed on behalf of the government. Powers merged with Remington-Rand in 1927.

Initial products from Powers were functionally superior to Hollerith's in a situation much like that often encountered by IBM today. However, Watson's skill in marketing and customer relations were able to overshadow Power's engineering abilities. IBM's consummate skill was in assuring customers that their data processing problems would be solved rather than in emphasizing the innovativeness of the technologies it offered. Although IBM had to respond when new technologies emerged (this is discussed later in the chapter), it kept the focus on customer support. Consequently, customers increasingly grew to depend on it. Still, Powers and Remington-Rand remained important players. On the brink of World War II, tabulating machine sales were dominated by both IBM and Remington-Rand.

Cortada concludes that tabulating machines were the real forerunners of computers. Unlike the cash register, calculator, and typewriter, tabulators were designed to handle large amounts of data. Eventually, in the 1930s and 1940s, calculators and tabulators merged as businesses needed to process ever-increasing amounts of data. Much more recently, cash registers and typewriters have, in effect, become computers. Thus, the four industries eventually converged into one.

Some of the reasons for this convergence are technical in nature. For example, keyboards became a common element in all of these business machines. Related technologies that may also have facilitated convergence were the telegraph and telephone.

Of course, a primary motivating factor in the search for synergies between the industries was their common audience. This factor was probably a strong influence in the merging of firms to provide a wider variety of products. Cortada indicates that by 1924–1925, twenty-six companies sold adding machines, fourteen sold calculating machines, eight sold bookkeeping machines, and six sold billing machines. However, between World War I and the end of the 1920s, there were many consolidations, prompted in part by the increasingly capital-intensive nature of the business.

We can see a consolidation situation emerging here across industry segments. Initially, consolidation occurred within each segment of the business machine industry, that is, within adding machine or typewriter markets alone. However, in more recent years, the distinctions between these types of machines slowly but surely faded. Thus, we now see most people doing their "typewriting" on personal computers rather than on typewriters. Consolidations, therefore, need not be restricted to a single industry.

The maturation of these industries can easily be seen as evolution situations. All of these business machines met with little enthusiasm when they were first developed. Many years passed before the methods and costs of production and the marketing techniques were sufficiently sophisticated to be able to provide value to the marketplace at a reasonable price. It was also important for them to demonstrate convincingly that these machines offered benefits in a sufficient range of applications. Such demonstrations were critical to creating a crossing the chasm situation. These lessons are as true for industries today as they were for these industries earlier in this century and for steamboats even earlier than that.

Cortada (1993) notes that the government and large industrial enterprises were the first customers of the business machine industries. They could afford to use new technologies earlier than smaller, private businesses could. But as use of these machines spread, customers became more knowledgeable and their demands for additional functionality increased. In addition, service and education were seen to be essential if customers were to allow themselves to become increasingly dependent upon these machines. Meeting the demands for greater functionality and reliability, as well as increasingly supportive service, required that competitors invest more to stay in the business. The inability of many companies to sustain such investment was one of the factors promoting consolidation.

Cortada reflects on the impact on the industry of people such as Burroughs and Watson. Although he concedes that they provided important leadership, he suggests that eventual industry success came more from a wide range of organizations and people who sought to find the means for dealing with the explosion of business information that accompanied the continual economic expansion and industrialization. In other words, according to Cortada, people like Burroughs and Watson were at the right place at the right time but did not create the times.

Here we see an interesting contrast between organic and synthetic views. The pioneers in the business machine industry certainly demonstrated their ability to synthesize solutions to increasingly important business problems. However, this process was driven by recognition of organic forces and trends. Further, the processes whereby they marketed, sold, and supported these machines very much reflected the organic nature of the marketplace.

Early Digital Computing

The emergence of digital computing and the maturation of the computer industry have been described by Franklin M. Fisher, James W. McKie, and Richard B. Mancke in IBM *and the U.S. Data Processing*

Industry (1983). A somewhat different perspective is offered by Norman Macrae in his biography *John von Neumann* (1992).

Macrae asserts that digital computers and electronic computing emerged because of twenty years of pure academic research in quantum theory that ushered in the electronics age. He also gives much credit to J. Presper Eckert at the University of Pennsylvania and to "one of the cleverest men in the world," John von Neumann of Princeton University.

The key sequence of events starts with John V. Atansoff of Iowa State, who built a prototype of an electromechanical digital computer in 1939. Other electromechanical computers include the IBM-sponsored Automatic Sequence Controlled Calculator (also known as the Mark I) developed in 1944 at Harvard by Howard Aiken, and a computer developed by Bell Laboratories during the same period.

John W. Mauchly joined the University of Pennsylvania faculty in 1942, soon after meeting John Atansoff, who was then working on a vacuum tube–based computer concept. J. Presper Eckert, a young engineer at the University of Pennsylvania, was immediately taken with Mauchly's description of the idea. Work started in 1943 with support from the U.S. Army's Ballistics Research Laboratory. The army was interested in faster ways to create firing tables for artillery use.

By 1946, the two had completed the Electronic Numerical Integrator and Calculator (ENIAC), which was the first all-purpose, all-electronic digital computer. Avoiding the electrically driven mechanical relays of the earlier computers resulted in a speed increase by a factor of a thousand. However, ENIAC and the subsequent Electronic Discrete Variable Computer (EDVAC) in 1950 were by no means immediately successful. Business—and in particular IBM—dismissed the concept as too expensive and too risky.

Nevertheless, von Neumann, according to Macrae (1992), saw the potential immediately, and his thinking quickly outpaced that of Eckert and Mauchly. Von Neuman realized that the essence of computing was the logical functions performed and that the necessary next step was stored-program computing. He outlined this next step in what became known as "the First Draft," which Macrae asserts "served as a model for virtually all future studies of logical design of computers" (p. 286). Working at the Institute for Advanced Study (IAS) at Princeton, von Neumann and his team continued their work on computer architectures. By 1952, there were seven descendants of the IAS computer: MANIAC (Los Alamos), JOHNNIAC (Rand Corporation), AVIDAC (Argonne National Laboratory), ORDVAC (Aberdeen Proving Ground), ORACLE (Oak Ridge National Laboratory), ILLIAC (University of Illinois), and most important the IBM 701, which led IBM into world dominance.

Eckert and Mauchly were not sitting idly by during this period. In 1946, they left the University of Pennsylvania to set up the Eckert-Mauchly Corporation. They built Binary Automatic Computer (BINAC) for Northrop Corporation in 1950 and Universal Automatic Computer (UNIVAC) for the Census Bureau in 1951.

Eckert and Mauchly approached IBM for investment capital during this period. However, fearing antitrust problems, IBM declined. Subsequently, they were bought in 1950–1951 by Remington-Rand. In 1955, Remington-Rand was bought by Sperry, creating Sperry-Rand. Thus, consolidation continued.

The intellectual relationship between Eckert and Mauchly and John von Neumann had long-lasting effects. Sperry-Rand brought litigation against other computer companies, claiming that they had appropriated Eckert and Mauchly ideas. These claims were dismissed in 1973 based on a judgment that the ideas were in the public domain because of the nature of von Neumann's First Draft. Another factor in the dismissal was the fact that the original idea was Atansoff's.

As this vignette makes clear, starting in the early to mid 1950s, the race to gain market share in the growing computer industry became increasingly heated. Remington-Rand was the first one out of the starting gate. As noted earlier, this company entered the computer business by acquiring Eckert-Mauchly in 1950. In 1952, it acquired Engineering Research Associates, which had been formed in 1946 by William Norris and others. Cortada (1993) concludes that consolidations such as those initiated by Remington-Rand were the result of low profit margins in an increasingly competitive industry. He notes that such consolidations exhibited a recognizable pattern first with typewriter manufacturers and then with adding and tabulating machine vendors. Such consolidations could result in economies of scale if marketing and manufacturing were integrated.

The patterns recognized by Cortada can be generalized to capture many and probably most of the consolidation situations discussed thus far. Such stories begin with a technology—usually after long evolution situations—becoming sufficiently mature to penetrate broader markets. This maturity involves not just the product technology but also the technology necessary for manufacturing, support, marketing, and sales. With all the pieces in place, crossing the chasm situations emerge.

Initial success in broader markets leads, often quickly, to dramatic increases in the number of players. Each one scrambles for market share, which may be a relatively easy task during initial steady growth situations. However, eventually market share comes only with lower prices and higher costs, that is, increased costs of selling, leading to lower gross and net profit margins. The subsequent need for capital to compete leads seemingly inevitably to consolidation situations.

Fisher and colleagues point out that in the case of Remington-Rand the benefits of consolidation were far from immediate. They quote William Norris: "Remington-Rand faltered at the crucial time when it had a chance to take over the computer market. The hesitation was the result of Jim Rand being too old to be able to carry through on a great opportunity" (1983, p. 38). Norris said that Sperry-Rand's failure to focus on the computer business was one of the reasons that he left to form Control Data Corporation (CDC) in 1957. Fisher and colleagues quote *Business Week*'s observation in November 1969 that Sperry "snatched defeat from the jaws of victory" ("Univac Comes in").

Remington-Rand had some early success, including selling UNIVAC machines to the Census Bureau where they displaced IBM tabulators. At this point IBM certainly took notice. However, as Thomas Watson, Jr. notes (1990), IBM eventually beat out Remington-Rand because the latter was more of a conglomerate than a computer company. Management did not put their money and hearts behind the technology.

Fisher and colleagues observe that Rand had no computer-related profit centers until 1964. In other words, it treated computers much like any other piece of equipment or office furniture. In contrast, IBM recognized the tremendous potential of computers and how they had to be marketed. In other words, IBM responded to the organic needs of the marketplace by synthesizing a type of company tailored to meet these needs.

Thomas Watson, Jr. asserts that IBM succeeded by focusing on deep system knowledge, which helped their customers succeed. Reflecting on IBM's success in overcoming Remington-Rand, Cortada (1993) concludes that "all available evidence points to the effectiveness of having a corporate strategy that works as opposed simply to allowing market conditions to control business rhythms opportunistically" (p. 150). He elaborates by noting that "abhorrence of reacting as opposed to responding proactively remained one of the fundamental characteristics of IBM's culture deep into the twentieth century" (p. 150).

These observations are critical. Fairly quickly—although not immediately, as the following paragraphs explain—IBM recognized what was likely to happen in the business machines industry and responded with a strategy that gave it a degree of control. In other words, IBM responded organically to long-term market trends by synthetically developing a customer-oriented strategy that helped its customers to deal successfully with trends that were affecting them.

This balancing of the organic and synthetic perspectives often is a central aspect to success, especially when a company is in a consolidation situation. In contrast, in vision quest and evolution situations, such balancing tends to be less important because companies do not have to deal with growing numbers of competitors. However, once they make the transition to a crossing the chasm situation, and especially if they eventually become involved in a consolidation situation, they may need the balancing skills that they previously overlooked.

Despite IBM's success, Remington-Rand remained an important competitor in the computer industry for quite some time. During the 1950s, both IBM and Remington-Rand prospered, as did Burroughs, NCR, and Underwood. This was possible because large organizations had an increasing desire to process large amounts of data in order to manage their enterprises better and because a relatively strong economy enabled investments in data processing equipment. Cortada notes that government funding of postwar R&D also contributed to the market. As a result, by 1954 there were twenty-three firms in the computer business, not counting the aircraft companies and the universities. As the indicators in Exhibit 4.2 show, consolidation situations would soon emerge.

Fisher and colleagues (1983) chronicle the emergence of new players and their consolidation during the 1950s and 1960s. Here is a summary of the events: In 1953, NCR acquired Computer Research Corporation from Northrop Aviation. In 1956, Burroughs acquired Electrodata. In 1957, Honeywell bought Raytheon's share of Datamatic Corporation, which they had formed together in 1955. In 1961, Philco departed from the computer business (in part because it had been acquired by Ford). In 1963, CDC made seven acquisitions, including Bendix's computer operations. In 1969, General Electric (GE) sold its computer business to Honeywell, based on the former's assessment that its product lines were obsolete and technical position lagging. In 1971, Sperry-Rand bought RCA's computer business, which had been in trouble for quite some time.

These consolidation situations were caused by missed opportunities caused in turn by outright product failures, the inability of some companies to transform themselves from electromechanical cultures to electronics, and a failure to focus on the computer business. By the early 1960s, IBM dominated the industry with almost ten times the computer-related revenues of the number two com-petitor, Sperry-Rand, which was followed by AT&T, CDC, Philco, Burroughs, GE, NCR, Honeywell, and RCA. Just a few years later, the rank ordering was IBM, Sperry-Rand, Honeywell, Burroughs, NCR, CDC, and SDS (Scientific Data Systems).

As most readers know, there was much more consolidation to come and several new, strong competitors entered the market. However, rather than simply list these events, I want to discuss the stories of IBM, Digital Equipment Corporation (DEC), and Apple Computer in greater depth in order to gain greater insight into the dominant situations that the computer industry has experienced.

In this manner, we will review three epochs of the computer industry. During the first epoch, centralized computing by way of large mainframe computers was emphasized. During the second, interactive computing with the much smaller minicomputers was key. During the third epoch, which is ongoing, the emphasis is on personal computing based on microcomputers. At the end of this chapter, I will briefly consider the nature of an emerging fourth epoch.

Centralized Computing: IBM

The history of IBM has been well documented by many commentators, several of whom were cited earlier in this chapter. Another important one is Thomas J. Watson, Jr. in *Father, Son, & Co.* (1990), which provides a personal perspective. This section of the chapter describes several developments in the computer industry from IBM's point of view.

For the Watsons, the history of IBM began with Thomas Watson, Sr. becoming general manager of C-T-R in 1914. Watson, Sr. had learned the concepts, principles, methods, and tools of professional, customer-oriented salesmanship from NCR's John Patterson. Watson further refined his philosophy and approach, and it became the hallmark of the company that would become IBM in 1924.

During the initial decades of Watson leadership, which included Watson, Sr. and later Watson, Jr., IBM was in the tabulator business.

The business grew dramatically. During World War II, the company tripled in size thanks to lucrative military contracts.

Anticipating the inevitable drop in military orders immediately following the war, the Watsons aggressively added sales capacity, enabling IBM to take advantage of the booming postwar demand for goods and services not available during the war. As retailers and wholesalers rapidly expanded their businesses, their needs for data processing also expanded. IBM was well positioned to prosper from this situation.

Watson, Jr. tells an interesting story of how IBM got into the electronics business. Until that time, tabulators had been electro-mechanical devices. IBM had been developing and evaluating a vacuum tube–based multiplier through its own R&D. This electronic multiplier was integrated into one of IBM's tabulators. However, because of the overall slowness of the mechanical systems in this tabulator, the electronic multiplier provided no speed advantage. Thus, this hybrid tabulator could provide customers no real additional value.

The younger Watson argued that IBM should put the product on the market despite the lack of additional benefits. Although the firm might not sell any of the systems, it would be able to claim that it had developed the world's first electronic tabulating system. The public relations value of this claim would justify writing off the investment made in a system that provided no additional value. As a result, the IBM 603 went on the market. In spite of everyone's expectations, the gimmick became a market success and IBM was launched in the electronics business.

In the 1940s, IBM had been funding research at the University of Pennsylvania and at Harvard University. As described earlier, significant developments in digital computing occurred during this period. However, the Watsons saw no market potential for computers, except perhaps in the scientific area. Watson, Sr. saw punch-card machines and computers as relevant to two completely different realms—business, and science and engineering, respectively.

The Watsons' view is not as surprising as it may sound. As far back as Pascal and Leibniz, developments in computation were driven by the desire to perform calculations involving engineering and scientific formulae. Many of the developments in the 1940s—such as those of Eckert and Mauchly at the University of Pennsylvania—were funded for the purpose of computing ballistic trajectories rather than payrolls or financial statements. However, the Watsons and many others were experiencing a crossover situation. Computing's biggest impact would soon be in business.

Also noted earlier, Eckert and Mauchly left the University of Pennsylvania to bring the UNIVAC to the market. By the early 1950s Remington-Rand had placed UNIVAC machines at the Census Bureau, displacing IBM's tabulators. This was one of many competitive challenges that propelled IBM into the computer business. In another instance, IBM learned that Remington-Rand planned to employ magnetic tape rather than punch cards as a primary medium. In response, IBM engineers came up with a magnetic tape–based solution, but Watson, Sr. rejected the use of magnetic tape.

Watson, Jr. was concerned about the wisdom of this decision. He asked his top salesmen if magnetic tape was the future and they all said it wasn't. He reflected on this experience in his book *Father, Son, and Co.*: "I was beginning to learn that the majority, even the majority of top performers, are never the ones to ask when you need to make a move. You've got to feel what's going on in the world and then make the move yourself. It's purely visceral" (1990, p. 207).

We can see the interesting contrast between the reactions of the two Watsons. The older Watson was determined to stay with the old paradigm to which he had made substantial contributions. The culture at IBM supported him in this determination. However, sticking with the punch card paradigm would have seriously held the company back. The younger Watson was not as invested in the old paradigm. He facilitated change in the right direction. In this way, he avoided a paradigm lost situation.

This story illustrates an important aspect of the vision quest. The keeper of the vision can lead the enterprise forward but he or she can also hold it back. People become trapped by their predominant metaphors. In this example, Watson, Sr. and others at IBM became entrapped by the idea that they were selling card processing equipment when they were actually selling information processing equipment.

The story also illustrates an important aspect of paradigm lost situations. When a vision quest eventually leads to substantial success, the visionary paradigm seldom continues to be the most compelling vision. Unfortunately, the original visionary may be one of the last to recognize when the paradigm has lost out to new ones.

This tendency is quite natural and common. It can be avoided or its effects substantially lessened by focusing on problems rather than solutions. When one is problem-centered one emphasizes an understanding of the benefits to the consumer rather than the technologies that embody these benefits. The consumer's needs and wants are likely to persist far longer than any one technology.

How did IBM catch up and eventually move ahead of Remington-Rand? A primary factor was its involvement in the Semi-Automated Ground Environment (SAGE) project at the Massachusetts Institute of Technology's (MIT) Lincoln Laboratory. The SAGE concept grew out of work during the late 1940s on Project Whirlwind. It involved computer-based simulation and was led by Jay Forrester. The U.S. Air Force decided to employ this technology to develop SAGE for its air defense needs. IBM was selected as the contractor to work with MIT during this development effort.

Until the late 1950s, SAGE computers accounted for almost half of IBM's computer sales. Thus, we see both the technology and market acceptance fitting into a story of evolution rather than revolution. We also see computers being used for technical rather than business applications. The immense business data processing market did not, by any means, immediately embrace computers.

As already noted, a key to IBM's eventual dominance was its commitment to becoming a computer company. IBM focused on fully understanding the technology and helping customers to gain the benefits that computers could provide. It didn't merely sell computers. It came to be known as the company that solved the customer's information processing problems.

This commitment helped IBM deal with substantial challenges. Reflecting on these challenges, Watson, Jr. (1990) recalls that by 1956 RCA and GE were entering the computer business. RCA was 50 percent bigger than IBM; GE was 500 percent bigger. However, despite their size—or perhaps because of it—these giants did not, or could not, make the type of commitment IBM had.

This serves as an excellent example of the organic nature of enterprises. Neither RCA, GE, nor Remington-Rand could remake themselves in the ways necessary. These diverse businesses had too many stakeholders with a wide variety of interests to be able to focus as IBM could. Yet IBM had little choice but to do so since information processing was its business and computer-based information processing was moving quickly. IBM had to move quickly also. A good example of IBM's ability to act quickly was their decision to abandon vacuum tubes and commit themselves to transistors as early as the mid 1950s.

Watson, Jr. chronicles the development of the IBM System/360 which was, by the way, the first computer I ever used. It was the fall of 1966 and I was enrolled in a sophomore Fortran programming course. Punch cards were the media. In contrast, at the moment, I am using a 486 laptop with enough memory and disk storage to keep me content. Clearly, much has happened in the computer industry in thirty years, not the least of which is that my laptop, as well as my previous laptops, were not produced by IBM. Development of the System/360 was driven by the need to replace eight computers in IBM's catalog with an integrated solution. IBM also needed a bold move to bolster growth and to compete with Burroughs, GE, Honeywell, and RCA, whose current machines were all superior to existing IBM lines.

IBM planned to announce the System/360 in April 1964, and it met this deadline. However, in order to do so some of the equipment in the showroom had to be mock-ups rather than actual equipment. Shipments of the System/360 began in 1965. Soon the backlog of orders became staggering and the delays mounted. However, by the end of 1966 production and delivery were proceeding smoothly.

Fisher and colleagues (1983) assert that IBM's commitment of substantial corporate resources to uncertain and risky investments such as the 360 is a primary reason for the company's continual success. Indeed, this gamble paid off handsomely. Just before the System/360 rollout in 1965, IBM had installed eleven thousand computer systems. By the time the 370 (the 360's replacement) was announced in 1970, that number had tripled to thirty-five thousand. Thus IBM's multibillion-dollar investment had yielded fantastic rewards. As Fisher and colleagues report, several commentators characterized the 360 investment decision as perhaps the biggest ever in terms of its impact on an American company, bigger even than Boeing's decision to go into jets or the Ford Motor Company's decision to proceed with the Mustang.

The other players in the computer industry had a variety of reactions to the System/360. Burroughs offered a new product line. CDC reduced prices. GE focused on price reductions rather than performance superiority while also investing in developing time-sharing. Honeywell focused on creating a family of systems. RCA reduced prices and announced a competitive system. SDS emphasized the product family approach. Sperry-Rand focused on leapfrogging the 360 in terms of performance. By the mid to late 1970s, GE, RCA, and SDS were gone from the market for the reasons elaborated earlier.

However, new companies began to appear with a totally new type of offering—minicomputers. DEC put the first minicomputer on the market in 1957. (DEC is discussed in the next section.) Wang entered the market in 1964. Interdata was founded in 1966 and acquired by Perkin-Elmer in 1974. Hewlett-Packard entered the market in 1967, Data General in 1968, Datapoint in 1969, Prime Computer in 1971, Harris Corporation in 1971, and Tandem in 1974.

Thus, an entirely new segment of the computer market emerged. But IBM dismissed and then ignored it. It apparently could not imagine that clients might want to do their own computing rather than have IBM support and possibly staff a centralized computing function. Although IBM tried to catch up later, it did a poor job of it. This is a good example of the course of events in a silent war situation.

IBM also had to play catch-up in personal computing (as discussed further in the context of Apple Computer later in this chapter). As with minicomputers, IBM could not imagine a large market for microcomputers. Again, it eventually responded with a competitive offering. But its success was short-lived as computer hardware, and particularly microprocessors, became commodity items cloned and produced all over the world in a commodity trap situation in which price was the dominant issue.

As the profit margins for computer hardware plummeted, IBM found itself in trouble, losing a lot of money. There were (and still are) profits to be made in software, but IBM's infrastructure is that of a hardware company in general and a direct sales and customer support company in particular. It is caught in a paradigm shift from large mainframe, centralized computing to small desktop, distributed computing. Many other companies have also been caught in this shift, including vendors of mainframe software systems for accounting, inventory control, and so on.

The result has been substantial downsizing for IBM and for the other remaining players in the traditional computer industry. Symbolic of this change is the end of the Watson line of leadership, wherein internal candidates were selected and groomed to lead the company. The current CEO, Louis V. Gerstner, is the former CEO of RJR Nabisco, the food and tobacco giant. IBM seems to have come to recognize the commodity nature and price sensitivity of its markets. It is difficult to imagine IBM ever again dominating the computer market as it did in the past.

Interactive Computing: DEC

The seeds of the development of interactive computing were sown more than forty years ago. Ken Olsen, first working with Jay Forrester at MIT and eventually with IBM on the SAGE project, envisioned people being in control of their own computing. They would not have to wait for the electronic data processing (EDP) function to process their requests and give them their results. They would see processing and results as they happened. Olsen's vision was a heretical one in the world of large mainframe computers produced by IBM, Univac, and Burroughs, and these players dismissed his ideas.

Olsen's vision resulted in his formation with Harlan Anderson of DEC in 1957. The formation and evolution of DEC is chronicled in *The Ultimate Entrepreneur* (1988) by Glenn Rifkin and George Harrar and in *Digital at Work* (1992) by Jamie Parker Pearson. The story begins with Olsen and Anderson giving up 70 percent of the equity in their company in order to get $70,000 in venture capital from American Research and Development (ARD).

ARD offered three pieces of advice. First, it cautioned the two not to say that they wanted to build computers because, as noted earlier, RCA and GE were both losing money on computers at the time. It suggested that Olsen and Anderson say instead that they wanted to build printed circuit modules. Although Olsen and Anderson had wanted to call the company Digital Computer Corporation, this advice led to them to name it Digital Equipment Corporation. Second, ARD encouraged them to promise more profit than available through investment in the big players. They promised 10 percent. Finally, ARD urged them to promise a quick profit. They promised a profit in the first year.

In late 1962, DEC won a breakthrough order for fifteen PDP-1s from ITT. With the introduction of the PDP-8 in 1965, DEC had defined an industry. The company grew between 25 and 40 percent annually in both revenues and profits over the next seventeen years. More than fifty thousand PDP-8s were sold during its fifteen-year life span.

I have a special place in my heart for the PDP-8. I did my Ph.D. dissertation using a PDP-8—serial number 50—at MIT. We had tape drive number 4. With 4,096 words of memory and 12-bit words, assembly language was the only realistic choice for my study of air traffic controllers' abilities to predict aircraft trajectories. A few years ago, my daughter saw a PDP-8 in the Smithsonian and found it amusing that I had once worked on a computer that was now in a museum.

Rifkin and Harrar (1988) discuss the origin of the word *minicomputer*. John Leng, reporting on sales in the United Kingdom in 1964, commented, "Here is the latest minicomputer activity in the land of miniskirts as I drive around in my Mini Minor" (p. 72). Thus, the age of the minicomputer was born. There were about seventy minicomputer manufacturers by 1970. Consolidated situations would soon emerge.

But not all of DEC's progress was as smooth as it had been with the PDP-8. In 1966, DEC engineers revived the defunct PDP-6 to create the DECsystem10, without Olsen realizing that he had approved this revival. By the early 1970s, the DECsystem10 was a substantial success, ushering many people (including myself) into timeshared computing. Olsen apparently had a difficult time accepting this new computing paradigm. Nevertheless, the DEC-system10 helped DEC to prosper.

In 1967, Edison de Castro proposed a 16-bit machine that was shot down by Olsen as too advanced. In spring 1968, de Castro left DEC with Henry Burkhardt and Dick Sogge to form Data General, which introduced a 16-bit computer long before DEC did. As a result, DEC's revenues tapered off in 1970 and 1971. Although many analysts blamed the weakness on the recession, DEC knew that its late entry into the 16-bit market resulted in customers going with Data General and other minicomputer manufacturers. The PDP-11, DEC's 16-bit entry, was two years late but eventually stood atop the minicomputer market with 250,000 units sold.

But by 1975, DEC's product lines of 8s, 10s, and 11s were getting old—only the PDP-11 was less than five years old. DEC's Gordon Bell was pushing the VAX line. Networking, via DECnet and later Ethernet, was the key to success for the VAX. With the 32-bit VAX, DEC leapfrogged over the competition.

DEC outflanked IBM by building small computers. Everyone else, including Burroughs, Control Data, Honeywell, NCR, and

Univac, instead tried to grab portions of IBM's territory in mainframe computers. However, DEC branched only slowly into commercial markets. It found that customer expectations had been established by IBM, which provided complete hand-holding services to customers. DEC was not prepared to provide this level of support.

By the late 1970s, DECmate was failing and Wang was walking away with the word processing market. Also in the late 1970s, Apple was putting the finishing touches on the first personal computer, which would spark a new industry. Rifkin and Harrar note that Apple's "opportunity was vast in part because DEC and Olsen, in a classic business oversight, failed to take interactive computing to its next logical step—personal computing—and thus left the field open to [Apple]" (p. 165).

Olsen stubbornly claimed that personal computers would never succeed. However, Dan Bricklin created Visicalc for the Apple II, and sales of the Apple II took off. In August 1981, IBM introduced the IBM Personal Computer (PC). The announcement rocked DEC, in part because IBM outsourced about 80 percent of the machine and, therefore, was able to enter the market very quickly.

DEC's fatal error was to allow IBM to preempt the marketplace uncontested for a full year. This disadvantage was made worse by the introduction of Lotus 1-2-3 for the PC. DEC lost about $1 billion trying to get into the personal computer market. Soon all non-IBM clones (except Apple) fell by the wayside. By 1984, DEC was out of the personal computer business and remained out of it for almost ten years.

In 1984, AT&T tried to acquire or merge with DEC but Olsen backed out of the deal. The introduction of the VAX8600 put DEC ahead again. By 1985, networking had put DEC back on top, and AT&T came courting again. It was estimated that DEC took $2 billion in sales away from IBM in 1986. However, by 1988 DEC was fighting Sun Microsystems and Unix in the workstation market.

By the early 1990s, AT&T had acquired NCR, and DEC was again in trouble. Distributed computing, based on low-cost, desktop personal computers made DEC an expensive solution. Severe cost cutting and layoffs did not stem the losses. Olsen was replaced by Robert B. Palmer. Still, DEC slipped from number two position behind IBM to number three behind Hewlett Packard. In the 1990s, DEC has undergone substantial organizational changes in an attempt to redefine itself.

What happened to Ken Olsen and DEC? Ken Olsen's vision quest eventually became a paradigm lost situation. There was substantial warning, however. Olsen's initial reluctance to pursue the DECsystem10 and the 16-bit PDP-11 are examples. His dismissal of the potential of personal computing is perhaps the most important. All of these decisions reflect a company trapped by its old paradigm.

Thus, it is clear that there were early warning signals for both IBM and DEC. Indeed, these signs are easy to see with 20-20 hindsight. But how could we have known in advance? At the very least, how could we have known as soon as the patterns emerged? What should we look for? The importance of addressing these questions illustrates why situation assessment should be central to strategic thinking.

Personal Computing: Apple

The discussion of interactive computing noted that Ken Olsen and DEC dismissed and therefore missed personal computing. Instead of DEC, Apple Computer became synonymous with personal computing. Steven Levy tells the story of Apple in his recent book *Insanely Great* (1994). The title reflects the ubiquitous use of hyperbole that was characteristic of Steve Jobs, one-half of the Jobs and Wozniak team that founded Apple.

Levy chronicles the emergence and evolution of the Apple Macintosh, including adoption of its features and benefits throughout the personal computer industry. This chronicle begins with Vannevar Bush's 1945 *Atlantic* article "As We May Think." Levy argues that this article and its vision of an information processing system that Bush called Memex sparked the chain reaction that led to the creation of the Macintosh almost forty years later.

The chain of events began when Douglas C. Engelbart read Bush's article while he was stationed with the U.S. Navy in the Philippines. Ken Olsen, and surely many others, were likely also aware of this article. However, Engelbart found Bush's vision to be particularly compelling.

Perhaps it was at this very point that a silent war situation and eventually a paradigm lost situation became inevitable for IBM and DEC. However, the case for this conclusion is difficult to make because so many similar visions were articulated in the years following Bush's article. Thus, it is impossible to argue that this signal event in 1945 was the key to the others' later problems. These companies actually missed many signals over many years.

Nevertheless, Englebart was motivated. In 1963, working at Stanford Research Institute (SRI), he published a paper entitled "A Conceptual Framework for Augmentation of Man's Intellect." The paper outlined his vision for personal computing. Within this framework, Engelbart invented the windows system and the mouse. He unveiled his entire system at the Joint Computer Conference in 1968.

Engelbart's primary patron for this work was the Advanced Research Projects Agency (ARPA) in the Department of Defense. In particular, the Information Processing Techniques Office (IPTO) within ARPA, which was then headed by J.C.R. Licklider, supported a wide range of software-related exploratory and advanced R&D. The seed monies provided by ARPA/IPTO contributed significantly to successful commercialization of word processing, personal computing, desktop publishing, and spreadsheets.

Levy (1994) contrasts the commercial impact of ARPA with that of NASA. He notes that ARPA's millions led to software products with persuasive impacts such as those just described. In contrast, NASA's billions only led to Tang and Teflon. Thus, the government's role and success in contributing to eventual commercial products is mixed.

I have worked with these two agencies for many years, most recently in advisory capacities and in the past as an R&D contractor. ARPA is able to get "more bang for the buck" because it focuses on seeding technological innovation. The agency is quite small—in terms of personnel not budget—and very lean, certainly by government standards and perhaps by commercial standards as well.

NASA, in contrast, views commercial technological innovation as a by-product. NASA invests most of its budget in building and operating space shuttles and, although its future is doubtful, a space station. With the exception of the much smaller aeronautics side of NASA, this agency's mission is to explore space, not to seed commercial industry. (The government's somewhat confusing role in technological innovation is discussed further in the context of the defense industry in Chapter Seven.)

ARPA's funding of SRI and Engelbart ended in 1975. As often happens when government funding disappears, the SRI team folded. Most of the team went to Xerox Corporation's fledgling Palo Alto Research Center (PARC). Engelbart went to Tymshare, which had bought his augmentation system. Engelbart's vision quest had clearly transitioned to an evolutionary situation.

The next episode on the path toward personal computing was taken by Xerox PARC. The center was established in 1970 to help Xerox gain advantage in the computer business after, as noted earlier, buying Scientific Data Systems. In the early 1970s, the Alto computer emerged at PARC. Alto features included WYSIWYG ("What You See Is What You Get") display presentations that greatly facilitate document preparation and management. The Alto also had a bit-mapped display that enabled its graphical user interface.

The Alto led to the Xerox Star, which emerged as the embodiment of the desktop metaphor. This metaphor would eventually come to dominate the personal computer market. However, Xerox would not be the beneficiary of this success. Douglas K. Smith and Robert C. Alexander in *Fumbling the Future* (1988) argue that Xerox lost a tremendous opportunity partly because of politics and timidity. Another major factor was the Star's substantial price tag: $18,000 for a basic model. Levy suggests that the lack of cost consciousness resulted when the scientists at

Xerox PARC proceeded as if they were working with ARPA grants rather than corporate funds.

At Apple, the culture was quite different. The ethic was, "If it didn't hit the streets, it wasn't worth doing." The Apple II was introduced in 1977 and soon became a hit thanks to its price, portability, and ease of use.

My firm bought its first Apple II computers in 1980 in conjunction with a project to build desktop training simulators. I can easily recall my first efforts with the Apple II. I had developed and evaluated a computer-based training concept using a DECsystem 10 as the computer platform. I read the Apple II manual and converted the simulation software to run on the Apple II in one day—that's ease of use!

Apple tried to follow the Apple II with the Lisa, introduced in 1983, the creation of engineers and managers lured away from Hewlett Packard. Lisa enabled direct manipulation, had pull-down menus, and employed icons on a desktop manager. If Lisa had cost half as much and been several times as fast, it might have succeeded in the market. Indeed, although we were committed users of Apple IIs at my firm, we never considered or even looked at the Lisa.

In December 1979, Steve Jobs and his Apple colleagues visited Xerox PARC. Levy (1994) concludes that they left with the paradigm that was to become the Macintosh. The Macintosh project was formalized in 1982, becoming Steve Jobs's pet project. Then, on January 22, 1984, Apple's now-infamous television commercial during the Superbowl launched the new product.

The Mac, with 128 kilobytes of memory, was far ahead of its predecessors but was nevertheless deficient. Its bit-mapped display needed more memory than envisioned. Fortunately, memory was increasingly cheap. However, these two considerations were overlooked. Furthermore, producing software for the Mac was several orders of magnitude more difficult than for less sophisticated systems. Easy to use, hard to program was the general conclusion, as well as the feelings of my company's software staff.

Sales in 1984 did not live up to projections. The shortfall resulted in a power struggle between Steve Jobs and John Sculley.

Sculley had been hired away from PepsiCo to serve as president, the idea being that greater consumer orientation was needed at Apple. As a result of the power struggle, Jobs was fired by the board of directors in May 1985.

The memory limitations of the Mac were easy to remedy. More important, in retrospect, was Apple's decision that its printers would produce documents using PostScript from Adobe. When Aldus's desktop publishing software PageMaker became available for the Mac in July 1985, Apple had an application for which it was worth buying a computer. The Mac became increasingly successful.

Other Mac applications that became quite popular were Hyper-Card and later SuperCard. The card paradigm and the ability to define links among cards to create what is called hypertext was pioneered by Ted Nelson. Interestingly, Nelson was another enthusiast for Vannevar Bush's ideas. Thus, the Mac's success was based on several innovative applications.

However, despite a late start, IBM was still the leader. IBM had passed up the chance to buy the fledgling company that later became Xerox. IBM had also failed to recognize the markets for minicomputers and microcomputers. However, IBM's PCs finally provided an excuse for corporate data processing executives to begin purchasing desktop computers. Although Apple had technology and ease of use on its side, IBM had the installed base of customers and relationships in the business world.

IBM chose Bill Gates and Microsoft to create the software operating system for its PC. The result was DOS (disk operating system). With IBM's huge market presence, DOS became the de facto standard despite an inferiority to the Mac's easy-to-use interface. At the same time, a commodity trap situation was emerging for personal computer hardware.

To compete with DOS's seemingly insurmountable lead, Sculley at Apple had to license the Mac operating system to others or lower the Mac's price sharply. He hesitated on the price cut until 1990, by which time it was too late to stem the PC tide. Levy (1994) concludes that this delay may have ultimately cost Sculley his job.

While the Mac faltered, the PowerBook, a laptop, was introduced in 1991. Apple sold $1 billion worth of PowerBooks in their first year on the market. The PowerBook concept can be traced to Alan Kay, who was influenced by Dave Evans and Ivan Sutherland at the University of Utah and Seymour Papert at MIT. Based on Papert's computer language LOGO, Kay and his colleagues at PARC in the 1970s developed the language Smalltalk as well as the concept of overlapping windows. Their vision of the ultimate laptop was called the Dynabook. The PowerBook emerged almost twenty years later, providing yet another example of a vision quest turning into an evolution situation.

At about the same time that Mac was stumbling and PowerBooks were booming, Apple introduced the Knowledge Navigator. Levy characterizes this concept as Sculley's personal mixture of everybody else's visions. In a brief but very compelling video, Apple painted the picture after laptops. At center stage in this picture was the Knowledge Navigator, an example of a personal digital assistant (PDA).

To focus on PDAs, Apple participated in the formation of General Magic, a venture with AT&T, Matsushita, Motorola, Philips, and Sony. On its own, Apple focused on the Apple Newton and related PDAs. John Markoff describes the evolution of the Newton in his article "Marketer's Dream, Engineer's Nightmare" (*New York Times*, December 12, 1993).

Markoff begins by recounting Sculley's sweeping claims about the functionality of the Newton and its likely impact on the marketplace. He argues that Sculley, who was Apple's self-proclaimed technologist, promised the market too much too fast. His eagerness also encouraged other companies to pursue competitive products much sooner than they might have, providing Apple with more competition faster.

The Newton started out in 1987 with a single engineer's vision of a PDA. A team was soon formed to create it. Markoff argues that Sculley was never able to form a relationship with this team. In fact, through his commitment to General Magic, Sculley encouraged development of a competing product.

As indicated earlier, Sculley was at this time involved in fierce price wars. Needing a new product success and needing it soon, he supported the Newton team in exchange for a promise to have the product in the market by April 1992. With only a two-year time budget, the team scaled back its vision. The original $8,000 machine was scaled back initially to $4,000 and eventually to less than $1,000. This scaling back required elimination of wireless communication as well as knowledge-based decision support. Only handwriting recognition remained of the original leading-edge functionality.

A prototype Newton was demonstrated at an electronics trade show in May 1992. It was discovered, however, that the language upon which the Newton's software was to be based had to be scrapped, causing release of the Newton to slip until summer 1993. In the process, many additional features were dropped. When the Newton finally appeared, even its premier feature—language recognition—worked poorly. The Newton soon became grist for cartoonists and comedians.

Initial sales of the Newton were very disappointing. This disappointment, in combination with the already mentioned hesitancy to cut Mac prices, resulted in Sculley's stock plummeting. He was forced out and replaced by Michael Spindler, whose forte is operations rather than marketing.

This case study of Apple provides insights into vision quest situations and how they can go awry. The Apple II and the Mac provide examples of visions realized. The Apple II was an unqualified market success, while the Mac did not meet expectations. Nevertheless, both products were thought of very highly.

When the Mac failed to sell in the volumes sought, the company had to scramble. Sculley's vision of PDAs was very appealing. When I first saw the Knowledge Navigator video, I was intrigued. My colleagues and I watched it again and again. As developers of computer-based decision support systems, we debated which elements of the Knowledge Navigator were just around the corner and which would more speculative.

For us, this video provided an important signpost in the evolution situation that our company is experiencing. In contrast, it appears that Sculley, as well as others at Apple, believed they could create a slimmed-down version of the Knowledge Navigator and quickly cross the chasm with this technology. The Newton and other PDA efforts resulted. The problem, however, was that Apple's technology and engineering skills were not up to realizing marketing's vision.

Nevertheless, I think the PDA vision quest will be fulfilled. Sculley will not be there and, at the moment, it is not clear that Apple will either. There will be many players in the game by the time that PDAs are ubiquitous and a steady growth situation has developed. Then, as usual, a consolidation situation will start to emerge. From this perspective, Sculley and Apple have played an important role. Unfortunately, only a few visionaries get to participate in curtain calls.

Levy (1994) concludes by noting that the lessons learned in creation of the Mac have affected the entire computer community. Apple is no longer doing the teaching. Further, the opportunity to capitalize on the Mac's superiority has been lost. However, windows, pull-down menus, the mouse—all are now elements of virtually every computing system.

The Next Wave: Microsoft and Beyond

Levy (1994) briefly mentions one very substantial beneficiary of the Mac's contributions: Bill Gates and Microsoft. As noted earlier, Microsoft prospered when IBM chose it to create the operating system software DOS for the IBM PC. DOS soon became the industry standard for PCs.

In recent years, Microsoft Windows replaced DOS as the standard although DOS was still there running underneath it. But with the recently released Windows 95, DOS is no longer there. Levy argues that Bill Gates wanted to replace DOS with Windows for two reasons. One was a genuine belief that a graphical user interface is better. Apple, with the Mac, had clearly demonstrated that this is what the market wants. If the Mac had been less expensive and perhaps easier to program, Apple might have had Microsoft's market position. Actually, the same could be said about Xerox. But Microsoft became the leader, not because it had the best product technically but because it had broad market presence, thanks to the IBM link, and because it priced its products more reasonably.

The second reason that Bill Gates wanted to replace DOS with Windows, Levy contends, was a desire to end the DOS era. Microsoft wanted to compete in software applications markets. With the introduction of Windows, Gates reset the clock in the applications competition. Everyone had to create new software packages, even the market leaders in word processing, spreadsheets, databases, and so on. The result was that several Microsoft applications gained significant market share, often bundled together as Microsoft Office.

Interestingly, the early versions of Windows were awful. Mac enthusiasts found great joy in making fun of this clumsy attempt to take advantage of features made popular by the Mac. However, release 3.0 of Windows was an instant success. Windows 95 comes still closer to providing the benefits of the Mac. Although it may still not be quite as good as the Mac, it does not have the price and programming limitations that have dogged Apple.

Today, most computer hardware manufacturers are caught in commodity trap situations. Software offers much better profit potential. I have worked with several computer companies as they have attempted to chart their futures. All realize that they need to place far greater emphasis on their software offerings and much less emphasis on their hardware revenues.

They all say this. Yet when reflecting on many of their "gut decisions," all that can be seen is hardware. They want to bend metal, not push bits. This comes in part from a desire to employ productively their investments in manufacturing facilities. However, more important from my perspective is their poor understanding of their current and likely future situations.

These companies have gone through vision quests, evolution, consolidation, and silent wars, and are now in the midst of commodity traps that they will not escape until they realize that they are also in paradigm lost situations. They are used to making margins on hardware and almost giving away the software, partly to convince people to buy their hardware. Now, in relative terms, people are giving away hardware. This requires rethinking the value and pricing of software. This, in turn, may dictate changes of the mental models that underlie these companies' financial systems.

These changes seem straightforward from a synthetic perspective. However, from an organic point of view, they are difficult to comprehend. Belief systems have to change. Hard-won skills may no longer be so important. All in all, such transitions are much more difficult to make than might be imagined.

Although software is now the place to make money in the computer industry, I cannot help but wonder what will be next. In a recent article in *Business Week* (June 27, 1994), Amy Cortese and Richard Brandt consider how Bill Gates is addressing this question. They outline Microsoft's efforts in consumer software, networking, and online services. These efforts are premised on computer and communications technologies becoming increasingly pervasive and inexpensive. Furthermore, these initiatives assume that everyone will view the services that these technologies facilitate as necessary utilities, like electricity, telephone, and more recently cable television.

In pursuit of these efforts, Microsoft's investments in R&D have more than doubled in three years. Now it has to lead. It cannot wait for IBM, Apple, or someone else to create its future. The software industry is already starting to consolidate and surely Microsoft will be one of the winners. A critical question is how it—or anyone else—can anticipate silent war, paradigm lost, and commodity trap situations. The obvious answer, from my point of view, is to use the situation assessment method this book describes.

Summary

This chapter explored a rich tapestry of stories from the computer industry. Over almost 150 years, there have been many vision quests, evolutions, crossovers, crossings of chasms, consolidations, silent wars, paradigms lost, and commodity traps. These situations have been elements in the overall story of the dramatic growth of the computer industry.

The chapter also discussed the interplay between organic and synthetic perspectives. Success in negotiating the many dangers inherent in the ten common situations requires balancing an organic view of market forces and trends with a synthetic approach to creating products and processes to enable a company to take advantage of market opportunities. If the synthetic view dominates, a company may become better and better at producing high-quality, low-cost products that are of diminishing value in the marketplace. In contrast, a purely organic perspective can lead to constant shifting of a company's priorities and severely limit its ability to make strategic and tactical decisions.

7

Defense

From Cold War to Broader Markets

The defense industry provides an important testing ground for the concepts and methods presented in this book. My experience with this industry includes several years as an employee at both large and small defense companies, a brief stint as an officer in the U.S. Air Force and, more recently, as a participant on several industry-related advisory committees and panels. My experiences have led me to conclude that defense companies are very different from most of the companies discussed in Chapters Five and Six.

What makes defense companies unique is that they have one customer—the federal government—although they may deal with foreign governments too. This customer communicates exactly which systems, products, and services it wants and then invites bids from providers. In many cases, this customer pays for the development of these offerings and assumes most, if not all, risks of the development. In return, this customer requires substantial purview into and oversight of its suppliers' internal processes.

The defense industry is a relatively new industry. Although arms manufacturers and purveyors have existed for centuries, they were small enterprises that tended to be owned by the state or the monarch for which the weapons were produced. The United States, for example, had arsenals that designed and procured weapons. Because they were owned by their customers, arsenals did not face the kinds of transitions that companies in the defense industry have to face today.

The modern defense industry can be traced back to World War I. The scale of that war was unprecedented. Massive armies were mobilized, as were whole economies of numerous countries and hence their entire populations. Until that time, the military's needs were usually met within the normal context of supply and demand in the broader economy. But with World War I, nations' productive capacities had to be focused on the war effort. The result was government-controlled economic and industrial policy.

This structure was almost completely dismantled after the armistice. However, when World War II broke out, many of the means of economic and industrial mobilization that had been developed during World War I were reinstituted. In addition, in the aftermath of the Great Depression, the United States had tremendous unused industrial capacity. It was consequently able to expand rapidly into military production and provide a substantial fraction of the weapons and munitions needed by the Allies during the war.

When World War II ended, a new military policy emerged. The United States did not demobilize completely. The postwar strategy was one of maintaining the capability to mobilize because of general concern about a possible World War III and particular concern about a nuclear war, which would leave little time for mobilization. The Cold War was on. As a result, there were substantially higher levels of peacetime military expenditures than historically. The military-industrial complex, as President Eisenhower termed it, grew steadily, claiming almost two-thirds of the federal budget by 1960.

Toward the end of the 1980s, the Cold War ended. By all accounts, we won! However, there are now strong domestic pressures to dismantle much of the military-industrial complex. In contemporary terms, many are advocating downsizing or rightsizing the defense industry.

However, there are equally strong pressures to maintain the status quo. Although the industry is only fifty years old, it employs millions. In addition, foreign arms sales are an important element in our balance of trade. Finally, a substantial technology base exists in industry, government laboratories, and universities. Government investments in exploratory and advanced defense R&D have, in effect, constituted the U.S. technology policy for decades. This country does not seem to know how to make public investments in technology without looking to defense as a primary motivation. In contrast, our global competitors—for example, the Airbus consortium in Europe and MITI in Japan—are skilled at making such nonmilitary investments.

Thus, decisions to downsize the defense industry are likely to have far greater consequences than simply decreasing budget deficits. Because defense has been woven into the fabric of our economy since World War II, we are faced with a difficult redesign problem. For many of us, this is an arms-length policy decision. However, for those involved in defense enterprises, this is a life and death issue.

This chapter focuses on the defense industry's ability to anticipate, recognize, and respond to changes, particularly in regard to substantial reductions in the size of its traditional markets. To an extent, these changes are different from those affecting the industries discussed in Chapters Five and Six, where I focused on the evolution of technologies and markets rather than the disappearance of markets. On the other hand, producers of canal boats, stagecoaches, interurbans, and mainframe computers have faced challenges as great as those faced by the defense industry.

This chapter considers the connections and distinctions between the defense industry and these other industries in terms of the situations they encounter and the ways in which they deal with changes. Essential differences are uncovered. At the same time, as was illustrated in Chapters Five and Six, the defense industry has had a strong effect on the transportation and computer industries. Thus it cannot be isolated as some people have advocated.

Nevertheless, the defense industry is different in one important way: its various elements cannot be examined in isolation. Government agencies are key participants in this sector of the economy.

Hence, this chapter also considers the role of the government in the defense industry.

The first consideration is how government affects conversion or transformation of defense resources (that is, people, technologies, facilities, and organizations) to serve nonmilitary markets. The chapter begins by considering defense conversion from the private perspective and then focuses on government laboratories—in the Department of Defense (DoD), Department of Energy (DoE), NASA, and so on—that are central players in exploratory and advanced technology development. These assets are critical considerations in defense conversion policy.

The government's role in this industry also is reflected by technology policy, both the de facto defense-driven technology policy of the past and the possibly more explicit policies of the future. The issues associated with technology policy illustrate the complex nature of change in the defense industry; a wide variety of important agenda items that are beyond the business success of private enterprises are involved.

This exploration of the roles of defense companies in particular and defense enterprises in general should challenge our ways of thinking about enterprises as well as our interpretation of the ten common situations. Specifically, the enterprises of interest include companies, government agencies, universities, and a variety of consortia. Consideration of this spectrum of enterprises will help us to assess the generalizablity of the situation assessment methodology.

Defense Conversion

During defense conversion, an enterprise transforms its resources—people, technologies, facilities, other assets, and the organization itself—from serving defense markets to serving nonmilitary markets. This kind of transition represents substantial change, often tantamount to a redefinition of the enterprise. As can be easily imagined, change of such magnitude can be daunting and difficult to accomplish.

Many authors have chronicled the difficulties experienced by enterprises in making such major transitions. John E. Lynch provides many examples in his edited volume *Economic Adjustment and Conversion of Defense Industries* (1987). He notes that conversion of defense industries has been a recurring issue in our economy, with both the Korean War phasedown (1953–1954) and the Vietnam War cutback (1968–1972) prompting extensive discussions concerning the most effective means for transitioning the economy from wartime to peacetime spending. We hear the same discussions with the end of the Cold War.

Lynch notes that these periods are quite different from that which followed World War II. At the end of that war, which came on the heels of the Great Depression, there was tremendous pent-up demand for goods and services. Many military plants simply reopened their prewar civilian production lines to meet this demand; this was termed reversion rather than conversion. In addition, the inherent temporary nature of the war prompted companies to plan how they would deal with eventual peacetime. (Remember, for example, how IBM planned in this manner, as discussed in Chapter Six.) In contrast, the military-industrial establishment did not view the Cold War as temporary.

With the end of the Korean War, unemployment in the United States increased to 5.5 percent. After the Vietnam War ended, it rose to 5.9 percent. In neither case did the federal government undertake special programs to offset the declining military market. In contrast, the end of the Cold War led to the creation of modest programs, through the Advanced Research Projects Agency (ARPA) and the National Institute for Standards and Technology (NIST), to motivate and assist companies to focus on civilian markets. In general, however, the reaction of defense companies to declining military spending is quite straightforward. When defense contracts end, companies simply scale back and downsize as necessary.

Robert W. DeGrasse, one of the authors contributing to Lynch's collection, defines conversion as "a process of adjusting to reductions in defense procurement that involves advanced planning to reuse, for nonmilitary purposes, a substantial percentage of the resources currently deployed for defense production" (Lynch, 1987, p. 91). In contrast, diversification involves entering new markets, often through acquisition, in order to decrease reliance on one market or customer.

DeGrasse provides an insightful analysis of how six defense companies dealt with conversion and diversification. One of the case studies is Kaman Corporation. Founded in 1945 to develop helicopters, 95 percent of its sales were in the military helicopter market by 1963. At that time, company founder Charles Kaman sought to diversify, and thanks to a hobby of his, decided to enter the guitar business. Such a transition seems quite a leap but it is actually a good example of a crossover situation. Kaman was able to employ materials and manufacturing methods developed for defense customers to create quality guitars in one-fifth the time normally employed to build comparable guitars. The new division of Kaman was announced in 1966; it became profitable in 1972. Kaman also subsequently diversified into the bearing business with considerable success. Although this diversification was successful for the company, only a handful of the defense workers and managers found positions in the new divisions. This is a very common result with successful crossover situations.

DeGrasse offers Acurex Corporation as a second example of conversion and diversification. Founded in 1965, this company focused at first on R&D contracts with the U.S. Air Force and NASA in the areas of thermodynamics and chemistry. A few years later, Acurex began its diversification drive by broadening to other government markets in the areas of pollution monitoring and control. By 1975, Acurex had launched efforts to break into the solar energy market. These diversification efforts involved technologies and competencies developed in defense work although only a few of the people working on the defense side of the company made the transition to the nondefense work. Thus, this is another example of a crossover situation that involved technologies but not necessarily people.

DeGrasse's third example is Boeing Vertol. At the end of the Vietnam War, this company entered the mass transit market. By the early 1970s, Boeing had received several contracts to plan and develop prototype transit cars. For example, it won contracts in 1973 from the cities of Boston and San Francisco to build 280 cars. In 1974, it won a contract to build 200 for Chicago. Unfortunately, testing was limited in the rush to meet delivery schedules, and many operational problems and penalties were the result. Eventually, Boeing exited the mass transit business. In this conversion, a large percentage of the personnel involved in building transit cars came from the aerospace side of the company. Unfortunately, this crossover was not a business success.

Raytheon provides a case study of successful diversification. This company first attempted to move into the television, television tube, and semiconductor markets through acquisitions. The acquired units were eventually divested, but Raytheon succeeded in crossing over the microwave cooking technology that it had developed. It acquired Amana and Caloric, crossed this technology over to these companies, and was firmly in the appliance market. It also built on its sonar expertise to enter the energy exploration market, again through acquisitions. This diversification allowed the company to prosper although few defense workers were involved. In fact, Raytheon laid off substantial numbers of defense workers at the same time that the nondefense units were prospering.

Ingalls Shipbuilding provides yet another case study. In order to reduce its total dependency on U. S. Navy contracts, Ingalls entered the business of building offshore oil-drilling rigs. A key element of its plan was the purchase of exclusive rights to build a particular type of rig. Ingalls also obtained contracts to assemble rail cars. These commercial lines of business allowed Ingalls to retain only about half of the workforce that it had maintained during the peak years of military production. Nevertheless, it provides a good example of conversion and another example of a crossover situation.

The last example DeGrasse offers (Lynch, 1987) is Rohr Industries. Rohr attempted to make the transition from aerospace subcontracting to ground transportation. Within a few years it had won a contract to build rail cars for San Francisco and soon after that for Washington, D.C. Rohr also acquired a competitor in the bus industry. This crossover situation involved transitioning aerospace skills in systems engineering, structural design, quality control, and fabrication from defense to transportation. But like Boeing, Rohr encountered substantial problems in producing acceptable rail cars and left the market in the mid 1970s. Both companies learned that developing low-cost, reliable rail cars is more complex than they had anticipated. I cannot help but wonder if crossover for these companies would have been successful if they had avoided bringing so much organizational baggage with them.

Based on these case studies, DeGrasse suggests that several factors result in the success or failure of diversification or conversion. The keys to success, he concludes, are leadership (that is, management commitment), technology transfer (adaptability of existing technologies to commercial use), market research (development of a market strategy), acquisition (firms or employees), and persistence (often a wait of five years for a profit). Factors associated with failure include unfamiliarity with commercial markets, premature introduction of new products before fully testing them, and inaccurate market expectations. Indeed, these factors seem likely to affect any crossover situation, even those that do not involve transitions from defense to other markets.

James Lawson, another contributor to Lynch's collection (1987), presents an analysis of market opportunities for the defense industry. He suggests that eight market segments are potentially of interest: shipbuilding, repair and production of aircraft, guided missiles, aircraft engines and engine parts, aircraft parts and equipment, radio and television, computing equipment, and measuring instruments. Based on a fairly thorough analysis, he concludes that only three of the eight sectors have near-term possibilities. The others are likely to require that companies invest five years or more to identify and redevelop themselves for commercial markets.

Lawson summarizes the prospects for defense conversion by saying, "History has shown that specialized industries that experience significant loss of markets often just simply disappear" (Lynch, p. 173). In his concluding chapter, Lynch is no less discouraging when he asserts that "Economic conversion has come to a dead end. It has never happened in the United States" (p. 219).

Although these assertions may be true in general, I do not believe they have to be true in particular. Building on DeGrasse's case studies, it seems reasonable to claim that defense conversion can succeed if the elements of a crossover situation are present. In addition, management may need to pursue conversion as a vision quest, keeping in mind that an evolution situation is the likely path to success. Finally, management, investors, and other stakeholders have to accept that a crossing the chasm situation is likely to occur along the way. Although the company may be across the chasm in the defense industry, it will probably have to act as a start-up in the new markets it is pursuing. The combination of vision quest, evolution, crossover, and crossing the chasm is likely to be difficult for many to accomplish. But it is possible.

Seymour Melman's *The Defense Economy* (1970) provides a variety of insights into several of the difficulties of this accomplishment. Melman begins by noting that we may assume that people who can design and manage the development of complex military systems would have the abilities and competencies to "convert, quickly, the physical and the human capital that they utilize to civilian uses, when that is required" (p. v). The remainder of this volume of essays shows why this is an unrealistic expectation.

In his chapter of Melman's book, Moses H. Harary discusses a case study of successful defense conversion. He observes that the company's ability to convert was not based on improving the capability of existing personnel to perform in different markets. Instead, the company simply withdrew from the defense business. Marketing personnel were replaced rather than retrained. In general, the investment likely to have been required to retrain technical, production, and marketing personnel was beyond the company's fiscal capabilities. DeGrasse would intepret this situation as diversification rather than conversion. It also represents another example of crossover with a minority of the original personnel.

Conversion is a much more difficult transition to make. Commercial investment choices are usually driven by perceptions of market needs which, in turn, determine the resources necessary—people, processes, and facilities—to meet these needs. Defense conversion, in contrast, starts with resources and then finds market needs that these resources can satisfy.

When defense conversion gets attention in the media, the focus is usually on the thousands of production workers and the hundreds or thousands of engineers whose jobs are in jeopardy. But C. R. Rydberg, another contributor to Melman's book, argues that retraining these people may not be the most difficult hurdle of conversion. Instead, the marketing function may be the most difficult to change.

Rydberg notes that roughly 8 percent of the employees of commercial firms are involved in marketing and sales while only a negligible percentage of defense employees are. The cost structures of most defense firms hinder such a shift of personnel, involving reallocation of perhaps 10 percent or more of a company's labor costs. Because the overhead rates of military companies are already much higher than effective commercial overhead rates, such a shift may require substantial downsizing of administrative functions. But such downsizing is impeded because most defense companies attempt to maintain as much defense business as possible while trying to convert. Thus, it is difficult to downsize or eliminate defense-related functions even though they will not be needed later. For this reason and many others, defense conversion may be more difficult than starting with a clean slate.

Another difficulty comes from the abilities and competencies necessary for successful commercial marketing. Commercial products and services must be more than just technically successful. They must solve business-related problems in an acceptable manner and with benefits that substantially exceed costs. Otherwise, profit-minded businesspeople will not invest in these products or services.

The difficulty is that military marketers are unlikely to be capable of understanding and communicating economic justification. This lack of cost orientation can result in a high cost of goods sold and high costs of sales. This usually results in high prices that price-sensitive customers will not accept, even though a performance premium may come with the higher prices.

Rydberg concludes that defense companies usually do not understand the marketplace or the importance of adequate distribution, product planning, and buyer preferences. Therefore, they usually find it necessary to bring qualified commercial marketing personnel into the organization. Also necessary for success is some form of marketing and sales support system.

These kinds of investments in marketing and sales are likely to be alien to defense companies. The typical defense customer provides information on needs, pays for R&D, and assumes most of the risks. Commercial customers do none of these things. Thus, the marketing function, and to an extent the sales function, must discover market needs and test alternative concepts for meeting these needs. This process is inherently much more expensive than defense marketing and sales.

Les Daly, a former senior defense executive, in his article "But Can They Make Cars?" in the *New York Times Magazine* (January 30, 1994) furthers the argument that defense companies are ill-prepared to compete in commercial markets. He asserts that the defense industry is "bewildered and frustrated by the insistence that they convert to doing something else—anything else—overnight" (p. 26).

This is an interesting perspective. It reminds me of a recent experience. I was sitting in an advisory committee meeting next to a senior executive of one of the largest defense contractors in the United States. Referring to the withered demand for defense industry products, he commented, "Defense contractors in Southern California are in a state of shock." I told him that I could clearly recall articles in the *New York Times* and the *Wall Street Journal* as far back as 1986 explaining that monies for new defense procurements had peaked and that there would be steady erosion in the future. Subsequently, of course, the Berlin Wall fell and the handwriting on the wall grew larger and larger.

The man responded that he and his colleagues had read all of those articles—but they had not believed them! They had clearly been caught in a paradigm lost situation. In his argument that the industry is being asked to change overnight, Daly appears to be caught in the same kind of situation.

The industry is not really being asked to change. Its primary and often sole customer no longer needs as many products and services. In such a situation, defense companies do not have to change. They can scale back or go out of business. Of course, quite understandably, they want to change because they want to survive and prosper.

A central difficulty, Daly notes, is the fifty-year relationship between the defense industry and government. The corporate culture of these companies has been tailored to that of their dominant customer. The result is complete dedication to high performance, with cost being secondary at best. Furthermore, these companies are extremely averse to risk, having become accustomed to their customers bearing almost all risks.

Bruce Berkowitz continues this line of reasoning in his article "Why Defense Reinvestment Won't Work" (*Technology Review*, 1994). He asserts that the Clinton administration's efforts to help ailing defense companies is good politics but bad economics and that the investments in the Technology Reinvestment Program at ARPA and the Advanced Technology Program at NIST are ill-conceived.

Thus, the problems defense contractors face are not technological problems but problems of management and organization. The highly specialized structure and procedures of defense contractors make it extremely difficult for them to adapt to commercial environments. Berkowitz outlines several idiosyncrasies of the defense business to illustrate these difficulties. Good examples are the Federal Acquisition Regulations (FARs) and the Defense Contract Audit Agency (DCAA). These mechanisms ensure that companies focus on cost justification rather than value. In addition, they control profits to be a percentage of costs. Thus, there are disincentives to decreasing costs.

Other such idiosyncracies include military specifications, also known as MILSPECs. I learned recently that the MILSPEC for chocolate candy bars is twenty-five pages long. There are also Certifications and Representations (Certs & Reps) whereby contractors must agree to comply with a wide variety of policies, many of which relate to economic and social factors rather than the product or service being provided. For example, my company sells software to the government. The Certs & Reps in our contracts require that we agree to provide this software with U.S.-made jeweled bearings. Our facility must also be certified as nonpolluting. Although this requirement makes sense in general, software producers do not tend to be high polluters.

Before we dramatically decreased our dependency on defense contracts, our costs of dealing with FARs, DCAA, Certs & Reps, and so on were substantial. When we shifted our focus to commercial products and services, we had to reallocate those resources to the marketplace. Government customers explain exactly what they want—they even publish it in *Commerce Business Daily*—but the needs and wants of commercial customers must be inferred. Furthermore, the inferences must be correct because, unlike government customers, commercial customers do not cover the costs of a company's mistakes.

Thus, Daly and Berkowitz and the other authors cited earlier make reasonable arguments for success being unlikely for defense conversion. In light of this conclusion, many have suggested a middle ground they call *dual use*. The idea is to create technologies and develop products and systems that have both defense and commercial applications. In this way, the government would get lower prices because development costs would be spread over a larger number of customers, while defense companies would become more diversified and more resilient.

This seems a reasonable proposition. However, there are difficulties in putting it into practice. For example, what specifically should be used in dual ways? Few systems have dual-use possibilities—certainly not tanks, missiles, or torpedoes. Many more components could probably be made for dual use. Good examples are semiconductors, sensors, and displays. At the technology level too there are likely to be a wide variety of dual-use opportunities.

The problem is that only R&D may be able to be broadly dual use. Some engineering and a little production may also be dual use. Systems builders are likely to be less flexible than component vendors. Overall, the dual use concept is a good idea but it is not the panacea that many people are seeking.

Richard Clark and Roy Werner address another important limitation to dual use in their article "A Better Mousetrap for Defense Conversion" (*Aviation Week & Space Technology*, February 14, 1994). They do not believe that dual use will become widespread. Their first reason is that military systems' long life spans preclude making commercial components with short life spans. In other words, commercial components go out of production because of slackened demand long before military demand for the same components ceases. Thus, the military will inevitably have to continue buying products produced especially for them. Second, the authors state, defense contractors are not in a good position to identify commercial opportunities and are in an even worse position to exploit them. These assertions are certainly consistent with our discussion thus far in this chapter.

Thus, Clark and Werner conclude that dual use will have little impact on defense conversion. My interpretation is that dual use may occasionally benefit the government, but it is unlikely to solve many defense contractors' problems.

Nevertheless, it is important to note that there have been dual use successes. Martin Tolchin reports one example in his article "Rerouting U.S. Technology to Travelers from Troops" (Tolchin, 1994). Tolchin reports on a government-funded effort that is focusing on developing civilian uses for the Global Positioning System (GPS). GPS is a network of twenty-four satellites that provides navigation information to American troops. It was developed by the

DoD at a cost of $10 billion. The goal of this effort is to make this technology available to aircraft pilots, motorists, transit systems, and ships. Soon after Tolchin's article appeared, the *Washington Post* (February 18, 1994) reported that David Hinson, administrator of the Federal Aviation Administration (FAA), announced the decision to adopt GPS for FAA use. Thus, GPS is likely to represent an excellent example of technology conversion. However, this transfer of technology does not necessarily portend economic conversion for any particular defense companies. It is quite likely that eventual contractors for the FAA will not be defense contractors. Thus, as with many earlier examples, crossover is unlikely to involve many people.

I have dealt personally with defense conversion on several levels. As already noted, my own small software company has gone through this process and has slowly achieved a reasonable measure of success. I have also consulted with a wide variety of companies, as well as government agencies, to help them entertain and plan for the changes that are evolving in the defense industry. I summarized these experiences in testimony before defense conversion panels of the Georgia State Senate (Rouse, 1993) and the New England Committee on Defense Conversion (Rouse, 1994).

I began my testimony by explaining that I have lived through two conversions—an unsuccessful one in the 1960s at a large electronics contractor and a successful one in the 1980s at my own company. I have found that there are three issues involved: technology, organizations, and people. Technology issues are not as central as often assumed. Technical competencies, for example, are often readily transitioned. In contrast, organizational issues are often much more difficult. Many market-oriented changes are likely to be needed, especially in business planning, marketing and sales, finance and accounting, customer support, and so on, as discussed at length earlier in this chapter.

The people issues are also often more subtle and difficult than anticipated. In particular, belief systems about innovation, technology, performance, costs, roles of customers, and so on often impose substantial barriers to change. For example, one defense company with whom I have worked extensively has produced one of its military airplanes for over forty years. Although the systems on board the aircraft have changed substantially, the aircraft itself has not changed much.

A member of this company's planning organization told me of its efforts to expand its production base. The firm was pursuing contracts to assemble elements of commercial airframes and other vehicles. But it was encountering some internal resistance from production workers. These workers wanted to remain in high-tech rather than commercial production. They believed that it was more "high tech" to assemble a forty-year-old military aircraft than state-of-the-art commercial vehicles. No matter if this belief was reasonable, it was governing their behaviors.

Yet despite minor technology difficulties and major organizational and people difficulties, I believe that defense conversion is possible—for individual enterprises if not for a substantial portion of the industry. In my testimony, I outlined six alternative strategies:

1. *Hunker Down.* Companies circle the wagons, keep what business they can, and downsize.

2. *Pac-Man.* Companies buy other defense businesses to gain a predominant share in their markets and ensure that they themselves remain players.

3. *Shotgun.* Companies broaden the market pursued to include FAA, NASA, NIST, and so on, as well as state and local government procurements in such industries as transportation.

4. *Godfather.* Companies broker remaining players and provide higher-level "value added" on large, complex projects.

5. *Cold Turkey.* Companies attempt major shifts to commercial markets while milking remaining defense markets.

6. *Cigarette Boat.* Companies start aggressive small ventures while also maintaining their defense business to the extent possible.

The hunker down and pac-man strategies do not involve conversion. In the former case, companies are likely to end up shrinking and perhaps going out of business altogether. In the latter, they join other players in a consolidation situation.

The shotgun and godfather strategies are based on the recognition that one of the core competencies of defense companies is dealing with the government on complex development projects. In the former strategy, companies attempt to provide their products and services to a broader set of government customers. In the latter, they attempt a partial crossover that builds on core competencies from previous roles.

Cold turkey is a difficult strategy to carry out unless a company has planned it in advance—or has no choice but to do it. Small companies, as well as younger companies, are more likely to succeed at it. The cigarette boat strategy can work for all kinds of companies, although its primary limitation is that it seldom quickly leads to substantial revenues. Although the new venture may be profitable fairly soon, the cash flow generated is unlikely to solve any significant problems in the company's core operations.

Successfully implementing any of these strategies is likely to depend on DeGrasse's key factors in success described earlier in this chapter, namely, leadership, technology transfer, market research, acquisition, and persistence (Lynch, 1987). In my experience, leadership and persistence are probably the most problematical of these factors, particularly in the cold turkey and cigarette boat strategies. They depend on transitioning to a new vision quest situation and accepting the likelihood of a new evolution situation. Doing this requires passion, persistence, and patience—all often in short supply when a company is facing the tremendous changes necessary for defense conversion.

The Technology Base

This chapter has portrayed defense conversion as a very difficult if not impossible task. Nevertheless, I think that it is possible for the hardy few. Success is attainable if a vision quest situation is pursued with a crossover situation in mind and with patient expectations of an eventual evolution situation.

Doing this may, in itself, seem rather difficult. Yet we now need to entertain a much more complicated view of the defense industry and its role in our economy and society. This more complex view is necessary if we are to understand the forces affecting defense enterprises as they attempt to follow the prescription just outlined. I begin this discussion by considering the notion of this country's technology base.

Government Laboratories

Roughly half of U.S. expenditures for R&D come out of the federal budget. Two-thirds of that sum comes out of the DoD's budget. This money is spent in industry, in government R&D organizations, and at universities. The result of this is the defense technology base that comprises a large portion of the national technology base.

Thus, the R&D infrastructure of the United States is intimately interwoven with defense spending, and these expenditures, indirectly at least, are intended to produce more than the results and products specified in the contract for this work. The nature of this R&D infrastructure was explored in a special issue of the *IEEE Spectrum* (October 1990), edited by Edward Torrero. This wideranging issue discussed a variety of critical challenges in R&D.

A long-standing challenge is to get R&D from the laboratory to the marketplace. Managing R&D with an eye toward market applications requires a strong understanding of the market's needs and an understanding of the players needed. At first, R&D efforts need people who are driven to find new knowledge. Later, they need people driven to create market success. Seldom are these two kinds of drives found in the same person. Although both involve vision quests, the natures of these quests differ substantially.

Another challenge is to provide evidence of the payoff. A study of eight hundred U.S. companies reported in this special issue showed no direct relationship between R&D investment and subsequent profit growth. Profitability and profit growth were found to be more highly influenced by good management and sales growth. Investments in R&D are, therefore, not purely driven by predictable and auditable returns.

A difficulty in proving the impact of R&D is the typical time delays involved: evolution situations are ubiquitous. Breakthroughs can take ten to twenty years. Many factors can intervene to affect a company's ability or desire to employ the fruits of R&D. Nevertheless, despite the lack of an explicit link between R&D and profits, few would argue for eliminating R&D. Most companies want R&D to be a vital part of their overall business strategy.

In the past few years, I have helped a dozen or so Fortune 500 companies do their strategic R&D planning. In all cases, the goal has been to tie R&D investments and activities to long-range intentions in the marketplace. Central to this planning, therefore, has been the creation of long-range product plans with explicit links to alternative enabling technologies. Corporate executives are reasonably patient with the almost inevitable evolution situations, particularly if these situations are pursued with explicit intentions of eventual crossover and crossing the chasm.

A substantial portion of R&D in the United States is conducted in the nearly two hundred federal laboratories, research and engineering centers, and test facilities. These organizations conduct more R&D than the nation's universities and employ one-sixth of all U.S. engineers and scientists. DoD laboratories employ roughly fifty thousand researchers. The Department of Energy (DoE) and NASA also employ substantial numbers of researchers.

In this context, an important R&D challenge involves taking advantage of the portion of the technology base represented by these government organizations and their personnel. With declining defense spending, there is a risk that the potential value created by these investments will wither. To take advantage of such investments, the Cooperative Research and Development Agreement (CRADA) program was created to enable companies to gain access to government technology for the purpose of commercialization. The CRADAs created thus far have received very mixed reviews, often because of a complete lack of customer orientation on the part of government personnel. Once again, government organizations are so used to being customers, they have never developed the skills or the culture to satisfy customers. Although their success, and probably their survival, depends on becoming customer oriented, they have little experience in it. They are very much in a paradigm lost situation.

There also tends to be much less market-oriented innovation in government because the government culture reacts more strongly to failure. Many industrial CEOs have told me that 100 percent batting averages mean that important risks are not being taken, but this point of view is rarely expressed in government organizations. They are not used to paying attention to market needs, even long-term market needs. However, they are very used to avoiding risk. Thus, simply creating a CRADA program is unlikely to be sufficient for success.

Leah Beth Ward's article "From Weapons to Widgets" (Ward, 1993) deals with the effectiveness of CRADAs. Ward discusses Martin-Marietta's (now Lockheed-Martin's) efforts to shift Sandia National Laboratories from defense R&D to commercially relevant endeavors. Sandia, at the time of her report, was involved in more than a hundred CRADAs.

Ward notes a variety of problems. One is the inability of such laboratories, and occasionally their industrial partners, to define viable target markets for their technologies. Furthermore, as just noted, the cultures of government laboratories are usually very averse to taking risks, which impedes commercialization.

Another difficulty comes in the form of the expectations of those companies seeking the labs' technology. They generally prefer exclusive licensing agreements because this gives them the assurance that competitors will not get their hands on the same technology. This is difficult to do with publicly funded R&D. Consequently, the focus is on what is called precompetitive technologies, although this focus tends to decrease the levels of commitment that companies are willing to make.

Overall, the result of these difficulties is that venture capitalists do not rush in to back new technologies. In addition to the limitations already discussed, venture capitalists fear that many of the technologies are too arcane and not sufficiently mature for commercialization. There are simply too many hurdles to jump compared with alternative investments. Although many companies would jump numerous hurdles if government labs were funding all development and taking most of the risks, this is not the case when the recipient of a technology has to make the investment and accept all the risks. This represents a new paradigm. Consequently, the paradigm lost situation is prevalent.

Considering what roles should be played by labs such as Sandia, Robert M. White argues for privatizing national labs in his article "A Strategy for the National Labs" (White, 1994). White, who until recently was president of the National Academy of Engineering, says that the goal should be eventually to wean the labs from government budgets. In light of Ward's report, it seems unlikely that the labs could succeed in such a transition. Although it may make sense from a synthetic point of view, the organic difficulties are substantial.

The greatest difficulty is that these companies would face the same problems as defense companies with even fewer of the competencies necessary to make such changes. As noted earlier, successful transition is likely to include elements of several situations— crossover situations, vision quest situations, evolution situations, and crossing the chasm situations.

Having worked with roughly thirty government agencies in the United States and abroad, I cannot imagine them successfully managing this magnitude of change. First, it is difficult to maintain and sustain a vision over a long period of time because elected and appointed officials turn over frequently. Second, there is a relative lack of incentives, monetary and otherwise, to motivate long-term commitments to change.

Industry and University Consortia

Several hybrid organizations also contribute to the technology base, including a variety of consortia that have been created to foster the transition of technology from R&D to application. The Electric Power Research Institute (EPRI) in Palo Alto, California, is a good example. EPRI was founded in 1972 to serve its member electric utilities. I have been involved in EPRI-funded R&D studies of power plant control room redesign, as well as development and evaluation of computer-based training systems. The basic goal of such studies is to leverage utilities' resources so that they all get results and technologies that they might not be able to afford individually.

More recently, I have been involved with two consortia in Austin, Texas. The Microelectronics and Computer Technology Corporation (MCC) was founded in 1983. MCC's members invested in its start-up and, in return, are stockholders in the enterprise. Members also fund specific projects that interest them. The history of MCC is chronicled by David V. Gibson and Everett M. Rogers in *R&D Collaboration on Trial* (1994).

Also in Austin, Sematech was founded in 1987 with the explicit goal of maintaining U.S. worldwide market share in the semiconductor industry. Until recently, half of Sematech's budget came from ARPA and the other half from member companies. Sematech is now totally member supported. Also heavily involved are companies that serve as suppliers to member companies. Gibson and Everett briefly discuss the origins of Sematech.

My involvement with these consortia has focused on planning to ensure that member companies find their investments and annual funding commitments to be worthwhile. This is made somewhat difficult by the diversity of members' agendas. Unlike an internal R&D function, there is no way to appeal to higher levels of authority to obtain a consistent set of demands. However, with appropriate methods and tools it is possible to negotiate acceptable R&D agendas.

Another type of consortia involves universities and industries working together, usually with universities taking the lead. Such consortia have been criticized for failing to meet industry's needs. This is due in part to industry not fully participating in planning R&D activities. Also important, I have found, is the fact that universities have agendas that they are trying to support through consortia that are not necessarily of interest to the member companies. For example, individual faculty members have promotion aspirations that involve criteria likely to be in conflict with members' interests.

Beyond industry R&D functions, government laboratories, and consortia, universities contribute to the technology base directly. Working with funding from a wide range of agencies—including DoD, DoE, NASA, and the National Science Foundation—and other sources, universities make substantial contributions to the national knowledge base, usually through publications. Thus, academia forms the important third leg of the R&D stool that also includes industry and government.

This industry-government-academia complex contributes to the creation and maintenance of the U.S. technology base. The Office of Technology Assessment (OTA) reported on a study of this process in *The Defense Technology Base* (1988). OTA concluded, "The technology base on which our defensive strategy and capacities rest is a dynamic, interactive network of commercial and military industries, laboratory facilities, subtier component suppliers, venture capitalists, science and engineering professionals, communications systems, universities, data resources, and design and manufacturing know-how" (p. 29).

This report suggests that two policy issues are central to this process. One issue is the extent to which government programs affecting the health of the U.S. technology base are appropriately organized, staffed, managed, and funded. The second issue is the extent to which government policies toward industry support the existence and maintenance of both the defense and commercial technology bases.

We have already seen that the relationship of the defense industry with its primary customer—the federal government—is quite different from traditional vendor-customer relationships. The government is not just trying to buy things such as planes and missiles but also trying to create and maintain capabilities to meet long-term defense and industrial needs. In the United States at least, defense expenditures serve a much broader role than mere creation and maintenance of military forces. Consequently, defense conversion has implications far beyond the problems of individual companies trying to shore up sagging sales.

Technology Policy

The policy issues associated with defense budgets, defense conversion, dual use, and so on are intimately related to the overall issue of technology policy. The concept of technology policy has long been eschewed by those who have argued that the role of government is not to pick technology winners and losers. However, the U.S. government's defense R&D investments have amounted to a de facto technology policy. Thus, the issue is not *whether we have* a technology policy but *how we can choose* a policy that is in the country's best interests.

Before discussing this issue, it is important to reflect again on the scope of the defense industry and the implications for enterprises in transition. It should now be clear that defense contractors in private industry are not the sole elements of the defense industry. Government agencies and universities are also elements of the industry. Congress and the executive branch of government are further elements.

In other words, transitional issues in the defense industry have to be faced by a variety of types of enterprises. Assuring continued employment for defense workers in all of these types of enterprises is certainly important. However, it is not the only goal. The long-term economic health of the whole country is likely to be affected by how all of these enterprises deal with the changes now affecting the industry.

Anthony DiFilippo discusses this issue in *From Industry to Arms* (1990). DiFilippo considers the political economy of the defense industry as well as the broader role of technology policy. He argues that a de facto policy that only supports technology through defense is dysfunctional in regard to overall national needs.

DiFilippo's line of reasoning begins with the assertion that economists agree that technology plays a major part in generating economic growth. Economists believe that innovation and improving technology are necessary for productivity growth, which is, in turn, central to economic prosperity. He also emphasizes the importance of investments in infrastructure, such as roads and airports, which also contribute to productivity growth. Military investments, in contrast, do not contribute to such growth.

DiFilippos's treatise is concerned primarily with the role of government in technology development and in particular as this role is affected by tax policy and R&D procurements. He notes that the U.S. government spends much on R&D but little of this money is linked to economic growth. His central argument is that the defense-oriented nature of the U.S. government's R&D program has interfered with the fundamental role of technology in promoting industrial efficiency and economic growth.

As noted earlier, military projects absorb roughly one-third of the nation's total R&D expenditures and a similar share of the country's technical personnel. This use of technical resources for military purposes contributes to a relative neglect of productivity improvements in the civilian sector. It also creates overall pressures to maintain defense R&D budgets merely to preserve technical jobs.

Military spending increased by 88 percent between fiscal 1980 and 1985 and was the primary cause of the immense growth in the budget deficit. As a result, the federal government crowded other borrowers out of the capital markets. Consequently, commercial enterprises found capital to be much more expensive than would otherwise have been the case.

Beyond shortages of technical personnel and investment capital, DiFilipo (1990) argues that U.S. management practices also contribute to our competitive disadvantage. Certainly, the hierarchical, command-oriented nature of many enterprises may be constraining. However, this has been an element of our business culture since Ford and Sloan, and a part of Western culture since Frederick the Great at least.

Probably the most important element of DiFilippo's argument is the simple idea that the United States has long had a technology policy despite continued denials of this idea. This policy has always had as its primary goal the continual creation of new, technologically sophisticated weapon systems. Great faith was also placed in the value of commercial spin-offs from this defense work. However, for many of the reasons outlined in the discussion of defense conversion, such spin-offs are very much the exception rather than the rule.

With defense spending declining, this de facto technology policy may cause us to focus on preserving military facilities and jobs when what we really need is a policy that emphasizes creation of commercial competitive advantage. I believe that the key to accomplishing this is to make U.S. technology policy more intentional. The de facto policy was always dysfunctional, but with defense spending waning, it is ludicrous.

Lewis M. Branscomb, former chief scientist at IBM, addresses this issue in his article "Toward a U.S. Technology Policy" (*Issues in Science and Technology*, 1991). He provides five broad suggestions that are intended to influence the process of policy formation.

The starting point, Branscomb argues, is a changed attitude toward the technical achievements of others. We have to get beyond the myth that all innovations happen in the United States. Consequently, funding is needed to collect and evaluate information about projects in Europe and Japan.

We also need to provide better access to science and technology information by improving quality control, adapting information to particular user populations, and disseminating R&D results. As Branscomb has noted in other writings, the United States is reluctant to invest in efforts to understand and integrate the results of previous R&D efforts. We have a tendency to focus solely on new efforts.

He also asserts that we need to build a stronger industrial base of dual-use technologies, including infrastructure technologies. As noted earlier, dual use is not the panacea that some maintain it to be, but it makes sense to pursue it where appropriate. I have been involved in situations where government sponsors asked for explicit plans for dual-use applications of R&D results. In these situations, having a good plan for commercialization of technologies resulting from defense R&D clearly increased chances of obtaining funding.

Branscomb (1991) also suggests that we should begin to focus on the downstream phases of the innovation cycle. Invention of new technologies is only the first step. To expedite the process of technology transfer, the subsequent steps of this process require careful attention. He cites NIST's Manufacturing Technology Centers as the types of vehicles needed to accomplish this.

Finally, he emphasizes the need to invest in human resources, from K-12 to the universities. Our educational system now emphasizes preparing people for college or graduate school. This only serves a minority of the population well. We need a system that serves everyone well.

One of the more visible experiments in technology policy is Sematech. Katie Hafner reports on this experiment in her article "Does Industrial Policy Work?" (*The New York Times*, November 7, 1993) and concludes that Sematech has produced several valuable lessons.

The Sematech experience has shown that the government should leave the management of such a consortium to industry, even though the government, through ARPA, initially provided half the funding. Hafner notes that two previous government-led efforts were disappointments.

An important element of this industrial management, Hafner concludes, involves having a leader with considerable credibility in the industry. In Sematech's case the leader was Robert Noyce, a pioneer in the semiconductor industry. With Noyce as Sematech's leader, it was difficult for the industry to not pay attention and participate.

Of particular interest, Sematech did not focus on producing leaps in semiconductor manufacturing technology. Instead, it emphasized helping suppliers to improve existing equipment. One way it accomplished this was to facilitate working relationships among semiconductor manufacturers and their equipment suppliers. Collaboration replaced arms-length relationships. In this process, Hafner (1993) reports, it was learned that "Saving the semiconductor industry actually meant saving the equipment suppliers that make the machines that make the semiconductors" (p. F5).

The government's initial support of Sematech—$100 million annually—seems unprecedented. However, there are many precedents involving much larger amounts of money. For example, the U.S. aviation industry matured quite slowly because of the capital and risks involved. (See Chapter Five for a discussion.) Consequently, government support was usually needed to sustain development of the industry, typically in the form of military procurements or mail delivery contracts. The government faced the choice of providing this support to aviation or allowing outright public ownership of the industry to ensure the industry's success. As a result, the government has invested many billions of dollars in the aviation industry.

The government also played a role in the development of the computer industry. For example, the U.S. Army supported creation of ENIAC, and the U.S. Air Force funded development of SAGE. Remington-Rand and IBM, respectively, gained enormously from these efforts. (See Chapter Six for more on this.) It could be argued that they would not have established early market leadership without having participated in these government-sponsored efforts. Consequently, the government's investments in this industry certainly amount to billions of dollars.

Thus, government funding has played a crucial role in the industries examined in this book. Clearly, individual enterprises participate in a complex socioeconomic web. This fact is nowhere more evident than in the defense industry. Indeed, it could be argued that the government is part of the defense industry.

This perspective is useful because it supports understanding the nature of the transitions necessary in the defense industry. The only transition that a defense company can make unilaterally is a transition out of the industry. In contrast, the changes discussed in Chapters Five and Six involved transitions within an industry.

Productive transitions within the defense industry require changes on the part of enterprises in industry, government, and academia. Procurement practices, cost accounting methods, and intellectual property rights concerns are examples of issues that have to be reconsidered across this multiplicity of stakeholders. Such discussions have to occur within the context of declining budgets, with millions of jobs sure to be eliminated and many others threatened.

The distributed, multifaceted nature of the defense organism makes it very difficult to synthesize new approaches. A vision quest like the historical attempt to land on the moon might be the type of catalyst needed to transform this complicated organism. However, other large-scale efforts like the space station, the ongoing major upgrade of the air traffic control system, and mass transit have failed to serve this role. These efforts very much represent business as usual rather than a national vision quest.

What is needed is something so compelling that we as a nation are willing to change ourselves to accomplish it. The vision quest needs to be so appealing that we are willing to cross over and persist in the necessary evolution. Perhaps a transition to substantial investments in health care or the environment could play this role. My guess is that the venture will have to be something concrete and focused for the nation as a whole to find it compelling.

For example, as a nation we might decide to provide computer networking services to every home, just as they now have electricity and telephone. Something equivalent to the rural electrification efforts in the 1930s might be organized to create the national information infrastructure or what is commonly called the National Information Highway. This would affect everyone individually and, consequently, might be able to gain broad support. It could become the vision quest necessary to motivate productive changes in the industry-government-academia complex that is now the defense industry.

If such an effort could be pursued with the explicit intention to convert the defense industry to nondefense markets rather than simply to build a national network, true transformation might be possible. But to do this, we would have to agree to stop fooling ourselves about technology policy. We would have to agree that business as usual is unacceptable. I admit that this is a tall order. However, we will not accomplish fundamental changes without agreeing to tall orders.

Summary

This chapter has served to broaden the base of case studies presented in this volume. The defense industry offers many examples of companies experiencing the ten common situations. Consolidation appears to be the default situation in the industry. However, vision quest, evolution, crossover, crossing the chasm, and paradigm lost situations are also frequent.

Change in the defense industry is most likely to occur when enterprises consciously attempt to modify their situation, that is, to change their relationships with their markets. In this industry, doing so requires enormous management commitment and patience. But there are a number of examples of successful diversification and at least a few of examples of partial conversion. Thus, change is possible.

This chapter has illustrated the role that the organic nature of an industry can play. The ability of defense companies to synthesize major changes is very limited compared with companies in other industries. The organic nature of this complex industry is the source of these limitations. The next chapter explores limits of change in more detail.

8

Changing Before It's Too Late

Creating a New Relationship with Your Market

The news brings story after story about enterprises delayering, downsizing, rightsizing—and disappearing. There is endless commentary about new roles for senior managers and executives and new relationships with employees, customers, and other stakeholders. Headlines proclaim that new computer and communications technologies are revolutionizing the ways in which we do business. Everything seems to be in transition.

What happened to the good old days? What happened to stable markets, organizations, and jobs? When did the crises associated with change become everyday events? The fact is, change has been a constant since the industrial revolution at least. In fact, the good old days also faced change. This book outlined the chronicles of the steamboat, railroad, automobile, aircraft, calculator, typewriter, cash register, tabulator, and computer industries. In these chronicles, we saw glimpses of the thousands of companies that appeared and subsequently disappeared.

It is easy to imagine the personal impact of such change. Millions of people saw their jobs disappear when innumerable companies faded. Thousands of fortunes were lost. There were countless crises as people tried to deal with change situations.

Do these kinds of crises have to happen? Do they have to happen to you and your company? There is no doubt that crises will continue to happen in general. However, they do not have to happen to you. How can you avoid the crises often associated with change situations while also securing the opportunities that they enable?

The case studies presented in this book showed that a large proportion of new ventures disappear or are absorbed by the remaining participants in the market. Why are companies unable to deal with change situations? The simple answer is that they usually avoid responding to these changes until it is too late to do so in a substantive way.

Companies are focused on dealing with today's issues and product lines. The short term dominates. They do not perceive situations as opportunities because they are feverishly working to succeed based on expectations that their relationships with their markets will not change. In other words, most companies are focused on ensuring that situations do not change.

When recognition of the need to change emerges suddenly, companies experience crises. They look for the quick fix, and such prescriptions inevitably arrive. When I began my professional life in the late 1960s and early 1970s, the key to success was called zero defects. During the 1980s, total quality was embraced as the silver bullet. In the 1990s, companies are focusing on business process reengineering.

For the most part, such philosophies are aimed at allowing companies to get better and better at what they already do. They emphasize streamlining, decreasing costs, and increasing quality. They do not, however, necessarily prompt companies to ask if they are doing the right things. They do not prompt them to question their assumptions about their relationships with the marketplace.

Cutting costs and improving quality are good, of course. But doing the right things is more fundamental to successful transitions to new relationships with markets. By identifying and doing the right things, needs to change can become opportunities rather than crises. The obvious question is, How do you ensure you are doing the right things?

How to Do the Right Things

To achieve success there must be a continual process for anticipating impending situation changes, recognizing their emergence, and responding to them. The capability to transform potential crises into real opportunities is best fostered if enterprises view themselves as in a perpetual state of transition from one situation to another, from one opportunity to another.

Continual assessment of changing situations implies other needs. First, people and enterprises have to be able to anticipate and recognize changes in situations. To do this, they must accept the fact that the ways in which they are succeeding today are unlikely to be the ways in which they will succeed tomorrow. So at the same time that they are taking the synthetic perspective—getting better and better within today's paradigm—they must also take the organic perspective—discovering tomorrow's paradigms.

Time is also crucial. If an enterprise waits until it is in the midst of a full-blown crisis, it is unlikely to have the time to respond in a way that provides it with any leverage. In contrast, if individuals encourage a response before recognition of the crisis is general, they are unlikely to gain broad support. Thus, timing of the response is as important as the speed of the response.

Finally, the methods of response are critical. Many executives and senior managers are reluctant to entertain situation changes because they are not sure how to go about responding to such changes. They have not developed adequate processes for assessing and responding to changing relationships with their markets.

The distinction between crisis and opportunity is also related to the time required for redeployment of resources. If a company has the time to reorganize its resources to deal with current and emerging situations, change can be an opportunity. But if there is not sufficient time to redeploy resources, then the need to change becomes a crisis.

Thus, to transform potential crises into opportunities a company must develop processes to deal with changes in situations. The situation assessment method is designed to help companies gain the time to allow for effective reorganization and redeployment.

The idea may sound daunting. I seem to be suggesting that you continually think about being different at the same time that you continually attempt to get better at what you are. Isn't this a pre-scription for schizophrenia? Won't the result be self-inflicted crises? Not necessarily.

Let's consider sailing as a metaphor for the process. At one moment, you are heeled over with sails taut and spray ballooning over the bow. But ahead you see the channel marker where you want to come about and head downwind. In addition, you see dark-ening clouds above. You think about when to come about, how to set your sails, and what to tell your crew—all at the same time.

All this book is really suggesting is that you think about your enterprise in this same way. First of all, like the captain of the sail-boat, you are constantly attuned to your environment, what is hap-pening in it, and what is likely to happen. Second, you understand the situations that are relevant in your environment and how you can recognize their emergence. Finally, of course, you understand your role in these situations and how you should respond.

At this point you may cry, "Foul!" You may claim that the tran-sitions we've seen in this book cannot be compared to transitions between sailing situations but rather to transitions from sailing to hiking to woodworking. This is a valid point, and it serves to high-light the fact that not all changes are possible.

Experienced sailors understand what is possible in sailing situa-tions because they understand sailing. They aren't merely tacking or motoring, they are sailing. Furthermore, they perceive the lead-ing indicators of each situation and know how to respond to them.

Similarly, a company must understand the market it is in and its relationships with the market. Is it in fighter aircraft, aircraft in gen-eral, or transportation? Is it in mainframe computers, computers in general, or information processing? The answer to this question will determine which situations are likely to affect a company and their implications for the ways in which it should deploy its resources. The answer also defines limits, as is discussed later in this chapter.

Sailing is again a useful metaphor because it illustrates how a company has to respond organically to its environment. Boats have to work with the winds and all the other prevailing weather conditions. They cannot simply crank up the engine and push their way through a storm. Such a tactic consumes many resources—including emotional energy—and doesn't work consistently. Consequently, good sailors continually update their situation assessments and thereby anticipate needs to transition.

My own company has been through two major transitions, so I am keenly aware of the difficulty of accomplishing them. We did not anticipate our first transition and experienced a crisis. We did anticipate the second, but it took us quite some time to develop and implement a transition strategy. Nevertheless, we avoided a major crisis and secured a substantial opportunity. Using the methodology presented in this book, we now focus on achieving transitions that are predictable and controllable.

How can you achieve this goal of predictable and controllable transitions? To answer this question, you need to ask once again a question posed early in this book: Why do companies fail?

The failures of most companies are the result of inadequate or incomplete understanding of current and likely relationships with their markets. In other words, they are unable to read the marketplace and the implications of trends. Most do not understand the current and emerging situations in the marketplace. Consequently, they are unable to make successful transitions.

To understand the marketplace, the three central questions of situation assessment must be answered:

- What is the situation?
- How is it likely to unfold?
- Which situation should be pursued?

The situation assessment method presented in this book provides a powerful mechanism for answering these questions.

The critical issue is understanding the situation that is being played out and probable future situations. The ten common situations and the forty-one indicators discussed in this book provide a basis for making sense out of a company's experiences. The situation assessment method also provides a reasonable means to project the future.

In addition, I have found that the ten common situations concept makes the inevitability of transitions seem less daunting. We all are participants both in our own stories and in larger and longer stories. One of these stories—or patterns of situations—revolves around your company and its role in the marketplace. Both the company's role and your role are likely to have to change as you make the transition between opportunities.

You should think of such transitions as normal and healthy. They enable the transformation and growth necessary for continued vitality. A lack of change and a lack of transitions, in contrast, result in a stagnant individual or corporate organism. Such organisms seldom provide much value added.

Limits to the Ability to Make Transitions

The ways in which situations are pursued have a substantial impact. The company's perspective—either synthetic or organic—will determine the approaches taken. Understanding these perspectives can enable more successful transitions and also provide insights into the probability of success.

The central premise of the synthetic point of view is that you can design—synthesize—an enterprise to pursue your mission, goals, and strategies. When changes are needed, you simply redesign the organizational structure, jobs, tasks, reward systems, and so on. In contrast, the organic premise is that you are but one actor in the social system of your enterprise and its environment. Although you may be a lead actor, you cannot fully control what happens or the evolution of the enterprise. You have to work within the values, beliefs, and preferences of other people and other enterprises.

Success in dealing with change is correlated with a company's abilities to balance the synthetic and organic points of view. This is because the key to enabling stable transitions and ensuring successful

changes is to balance responsiveness to the marketplace and continuity of competencies. A good way of characterizing the necessary
balance is to think in terms of the enterprise being driven organically
but responding synthetically.

Limits are encountered when the two perspectives are not bal-
anced successfully. For example, many companies attempt to make
major changes in the marketplace while also trying to minimize the
changes they make within themselves. In this way, the internal
nature of the enterprise, particularly in terms of its proclivities for
synthesis, drives the manner in which the marketplace is addressed.
As the case studies repeatedly illustrate, especially for defense companies, this approach seldom works.

The frequency of such failures begs a basic question. Can enterprises really change? An enterprise has psychological, social, cultural, and political attributes that cannot be reconfigured arbitrarily.
Therefore, a company's nature may limit its abilities to synthesize
appropriate responses to a changing environment.

Highly specialized yet very successful companies may themselves be their greatest barrier to change, despite successful track
records. They may have significant market insights and carefully
developed plans for pursuing these market opportunities. Yet they
may be trapped by their competencies.

Companies are often trapped in this way because of their underlying belief systems about customers, technology, performance, cost,
service, and so on. Belief systems that may have been central to success in one domain—for instance, defense contracting—may be
substantial barriers to success in others—for example, consumer
electronics. Companies are especially likely to be trapped in this
way when they do not even realize that they have belief systems or
do not understand the nature of their beliefs.

Yet belief systems strongly influence everyone's assumptions
even though they are seldom explicit. Our belief systems have a
substantial impact on our expectations, our observations, our
attempts to explain our observations, and our perceived courses of
action. Corporate belief systems tend to create substantial forces

that focus on optimization within the dominant paradigm. When the paradigm has to change, these forces can impose great barriers.

Thus, change usually requires much more effort than anticipated. Many people in a company may have difficulty understanding, or at least internalizing, the need for change. They may not understand what their new roles will be if the paradigm changes, or they may understand and agree with the changes but have no confidence that the enterprise can succeed in making them. As a result, widespread commitment to change is undermined.

No matter how well a company plans, it cannot transform an armadillo into an antelope. The synthetic point of view implies that an armadillo can be disassembled—its parts and genetic code restructured—and reassembled as an antelope. The organic model argues against this possibility because the whole armadillo must be dealt with: its biology, psychology, sociology, culture, and so on.

Clearly, some changes are unlikely to succeed. We would certainly like to avoid attempting these types of changes. Although I can offer no definitive rules for identifying such changes, a few indicators can portend difficulties.

First, if a company's current belief system is substantially different from what it will have to be after a transition, it may not be wise to attempt the transition. If the new situations being entertained do not contain elements in a company's repertoire of previously experienced situations, the likelihood of success is also diminished.

These two indicators are correlated with the extent to which members of an enterprise are confused and puzzled by the alternatives being considered. Such circumstances mean that the company should proceed carefully; however, they do not necessarily preclude proceeding. But the company will have to pay close attention to the five key rules of thumb, reviewed later in this chapter.

Defense companies provide the best examples of limits to change. Their ability to synthesize major change is limited compared with companies in many other industries. The very nature of this complex industry is the source of their limits. Defense companies are highly attuned to dealing with one customer, pushing technology, and avoiding risk. Their nature severely limits their ability to make the transition to situations where such characteristics are not useful and are even harmful. The distributed, multifaceted nature of the defense organism also makes it very difficult for it to synthesize new approaches. The interconnected network of defense prime contractors and subcontractors, government laboratories, and universities serves to reinforce the cultural characteristics of this industry. It also has resulted in a large number of enterprises scurrying about in the hopes of finding some way—any way—to replace lost revenues. I find that these enterprises are primarily confusing each other with this helter skelter search for alternatives.

Perhaps enterprises should be viewed as simply convenient packages of resources and capabilities that serve a purpose, in some cases for a long time and in many others for a much shorter time. According to this view, many defense enterprises have already served their purpose and should, perhaps, simply disappear. However, although we may no longer need most of these enterprises, we do need their resources.

Many of the country's scientists and engineers are employed by the network of defense enterprises. Rather than investing in airplanes and submarines that we do not need, this country should focus on assisting transitions of individuals and perhaps companies, government laboratories, and universities to more productive and valuable endeavors. The difficulty, of course, is that this will require much more time and create much more disruption than simply procuring more military R&D. A technology policy that is explicitly oriented toward competitiveness would help in this regard.

Defense companies and their special circumstances aside, how can individual companies deal with the limits of change outlined in this book? What should they do? Give up? Withdrawing from markets, disinvesting, and just closing down are real possibilities and represent the course of action taken by many enterprises. However, before such drastic decisions are made, a few additional aspects of successful transitions should be considered.

Beyond Methods

Although the method presented in this book can be of great assistance for enterprises in transition, several additional considerations can help determine whether a particular transition is a good choice. These considerations can be summed up with the five rules of thumb for successful transitions shown in Exhibit 8.1.

The first rule concerns leadership of top management. Is it committed to a new vision quest? The quest needs to involve total commitment to adding value in the marketplace in new and specific ways. It needs to have "a fire in the belly" that enables it to make the vision compelling to all stakeholders. If the quest is simply to shore up sagging sales and assure achievement of quarterly earnings targets, the likelihood of long-term success is substantially diminished.

The second rule concerns knowledge of markets and innovation processes necessary for crossing the chasm. Management must be committed to gaining the knowledge and skills that will enable the company to become a new company. This may require substantial

EXHIBIT 8.1. Five Rules of Thumb for Successful Transitions.

1. Commitment:	Top management must be completely committed to a new vision quest situation.
2. Investment:	Resources must be invested to gain the knowledge and skills necessary to enable an eventual crossing the chasm situation.
3. Resolve:	Transition to a crossover situation should only include those technologies and processes that provide competitive advantage.
4. Acquisition:	Transition to a crossover situation is also likely to involve acquiring additional key technologies and people from outside.
5. Patience:	Investors, management, and other stakeholders must be patient with a likely evolution situation.

investment of both money and time. These investments are necessary because the goal is to change the company, not just its markets.

The next rule concerns identifying and facilitating crossover of
key enabling technologies and processes. It is best if the company
can identify unique forms of value or unique ways of adding value
that will compensate for its newness to the market. Success is likely
to depend on crossing over to the new market with a few good things
rather than with all the old baggage. Much of the old enterprise—
including perhaps many of the people—is unlikely to cross over.

The fourth rule concerns crossover that must also originate outside of the company. It is very rare for a company to be able to make
a transition with only the personnel, processes, and technologies
that it had before it started the transition process. Acquisitions of
key individuals and technologies will likely be needed. Whole firms
may have to be acquired. Such acquisitions may be needed to create the critical mass necessary to achieve successful change.

The final rule concerns management and investor patience and
persistence. There may be a wait of five or more years before substantial profits are achieved. This kind of wait requires stakeholders to
commit to an evolution situation and recognize that the new venture
will not quickly replace falling sales in the traditional businesses. This
recognition may severely dampen many stakeholders' enthusiasm.

If the transitions that you envision can rely on this kind of support, then you may be able to overcome many limits. Although you
may not be able to transform an armadillo into an antelope, you
may be able to create a very fast armadillo that will surprise many
of your competitors.

The Role of Leadership

What is your role in the transitions that your company will make?
As senior manager or executive, what role should you play? Obviously, the most appealing role is that of hero. But are heroes really
necessary? In other words, do leaders make the times or do times
make the leaders?

The case studies profiled many very interesting individuals: Ford, Sloan, Vanderbilt, Morgan, Northrop, Sikorsky, Watson, Olsen, and many others come to mind. These people were persistent, patient, and passionate in their quests. But were they absolutely necessary? Would we still be riding horses and using abacuses today if these people hadn't lived?

In light of the rich history of technology portrayed in the case studies, the answer to this question has to be a categorical, No! Nevertheless, I do believe that these people affected the timing of the developments and the companies (and countries) that benefited from the resulting markets. These people did not make the times but they certainly took advantage of them. Thus, their leadership was very important.

We tend to think of such people as heroes. In fact, we seem to need to think of them as heroes. Occasionally, they see themselves as heroes. However, I think that they are better characterized as agents of change, and I believe that most of them would agree.

Many of us have a romantic notion of effective leadership as heroes leading charges. It would be helpful to transform our thinking to emphasize change agents whose roles are to facilitate communication, cooperation, and collaboration. Skillful agents of change know how to assess and create the appropriate balance between synthetic and organic perspectives. They understand the extent to which a company can adapt to market forces and how to take advantage of a company's abilities to synthesize. They know how to create transition strategies and articulate them in ways that are acceptable within both old and new belief systems. In general, they are able to "sell" change.

Above all, change agents understand the inevitability and desirability of change. They can see how bleak the future will probably be if the prospects of change are discounted. This understanding enables them to perceive leading indicators and the situations they portend. In this way, change agents are able to find opportunities among the many potential crises of change.

References

Barker, J. A. (1993). *Paradigms: The business of discovering the future*. New York: HarperCollins.

Berkowitz, B. D. (1994). Why defense reinvestment won't work. *Technology Review, 97*(5), 52–60

Branscomb, L. M. (1991, Summer). Toward a U.S. technology policy. *Issues in Science and Technology*, 50–55.

Bush, V. (1945, July). As we may think. *Atlantic*, 101–108.

Casti, J. (1989). *Paradigms lost: Images of man in the mirror of science*. New York: Morrow.

Chandler, A. D., Jr. (Ed.). (1965). *The railroads: The nation's first big business*. New York: Harcourt, Brace, & World.

Clark, R., & Werner, R. (1994, February 14). A better mousetrap for defense conversion. *Aviation Week & Space Technology*, 66.

Collins, J. C., & Porras, J. I. (1994). *Built to last: Successful habits of visionary companies*. New York: HarperCollins.

Cortada, J. W. (1993). *Before the computer: IBM, NCR, Burroughs, and Remington Rand and the industry they created, 1865–1956*. Princeton, NJ: Princeton University Press.

Cortese, A., & Brandt, R. (1994, June 27). Bill Gates: The next generation. *Business Week*, 56–62.

Daly, L. (1994, January 30). But can they make cars? *The New York Times Magazine*, 26–27.

DiFilippo, A. (1990). *From industry to arms: The political economy of high technology*. New York: Greenwood Press.

Drucker, P. F. (1994, September-October). The theory of business. *Harvard Business Review*, 95–104.

Dunbaugh, E. L. (1992). *Night boat to New England: 1815–1900*. New York: Greenwood Press.

Englebart, D. C. (1963). A conceptual framework for augmentation of man's intellect. In D. W. Howerton & D. C. Weeks (Eds.), *Vistas in information processing*. Washington, DC: Spartan Books.

Fisher, F. M., McKie, J. W., & Mancke, R. B. (1983). *IBM and the U.S. data processing industry: An economic history*. New York: Praeger.

Gibson, D. V., & Rogers, E. M. (1994). *R&D collaboration on trial: The Microelectronics and Computer Technology Corporation*. Boston, MA: Harvard Business School Press.

Hafner, K. (1993, November 7). Does industrial policy work? Lessons from Sematech. *The New York Times*, F5.

Heppenheimer, T. A. (1993, Fall). The jet plane is born. *Invention & Technology*, 44–56.

Heppenheimer, T. A. (1994, Winter). The dream of the flying wing. *Invention & Technology*, 55–63.

Hilton, G. W. (1993, Spring). The wrong track. *Invention & Technology*, 46–54.

Jensen, O. (1975). *Railroads in America*. New York: American Heritage.

Levy, S. (1994). *Insanely great: The life and times of Macintosh, the computer that changed everything*. New York: Viking.

Lynch, J. E. (Ed.). (1987). *Economic adjustment and conversion of defense industries*. Boulder, CO: Westview Press.

Macrae, N. (1992). *John von Neumann: The scientific genius who pioneered the modern computer, game theory, nuclear deterrence, and much more*. New York: Pantheon.

Magaziner, I., & Patinkin, M. (1989). *The silent war*. New York: Random House.

Markoff, J. (1993, December 12). Marketer's dream, engineer's nightmare. *The New York Times*.

Melman, S. (Ed.). (1970). *The defense economy: Conversion of industries and occupations to civilian needs*. New York: Praeger.

Moore, G. A. (1991). *Crossing the chasm: Marketing and selling technology products to mainstream customers*. New York: HarperCollins.

Morgan, G. (1986). *Images of organization*. Newbury Park, CA: Sage Publications.

Office of Technology Assessment. (1988). *The defense technology base*. Washington, DC: U.S. Government Printing Office.

Pearson, J. P. (Ed.). (1992). *Digital at work: Snapshots from the first thirty-five years*. Maynard, MA: Digital Press.

Rae, J. B. (1968). *Climb to greatness: The American aircraft industry, 1920–1960*. Cambridge, MA: MIT Press.

Rifkin, G., & Harrar, G. (1988). *The ultimate entrepreneur: The story of Ken Olsen and Digital Equipment Corporation*. Chicago: Contemporary Books.

Rosenblatt, R. (1983, July 3). Machine of the year. *Time Magazine*, 12–13.

Rouse, W. B. (1993, October 20). Defense conversion. *Testimony before Georgia Senate Study Committee on Defense Conversion Strategies*, Atlanta, GA.

Rouse, W. B. (1994, November 11). Defense conversion. *Presentation to the New England Committee on Defense Conversion*, Hartford, CT.

Schwartz, P. (1991). *The art of the long view: Planning for the future in an uncertain world*. New York: Doubleday.

Smith, D. K., & Alexander, R. C. (1988). *Fumbling the future: How Xerox invented, then ignored, the first personal computer*. New York: Morrow.

Staudenmaier, J. (1994, Fall). Henry Ford's big flaw. *Invention & Technology*, 34–44.

Tolchin, M. (1994, February 14). Rerouting U.S. technology from travelers to troops. *The New York Times*, A6.

Torrero, E. (Ed.). (1990). Special issue on R&D. *IEEE Spectrum, 27*(10), 25–84.

Univac comes in from the cold. (1969, November 22). *Business Week*, 160–163.

Ward, L. B. (1993, October 24). From weapons to widgets. *The New York Times*, F5.

Watson, T. J., Jr. (1990). *Father, son, & co*. New York: Bantam Books.

White, N. (1993, Fall). From tractor to tank. *Invention & Technology*, 58–63.

White, R. M. (1994). A strategy for the national labs. *Technology Review*, 69.

Wilson, J. R. (1994, September). Boeing restructures for future uncertainties. *Interavia*, 23–26.

Wohleber, C. (1993, Winter). Straight up. *Invention & Technology*, 26–38.

Womack, J. P., Jones, D. T., & Roos, D. (1991). *The machine that changed the world: The story of lean production*. New York: HarperCollins.

Zellner, W., Hof, R. D., Brandt, R., Baker, S., & Greising, D. (1995, February 9). Go-go giants: These giants keep expanding—just like scrappy startups. *Business Week*, 64–70.

Index

A

Aiken, H., 142

Airbus, 130

Aircraft industry, 122–132; consolidation business situations in, 126–127, 131–133; crossing the chasm business situation in, 124; evolution business situations in, 122–123, 127–129, 132; limits to change in, 68–69; paradigm lost business situations in, 42, 68, 126; silent war business situations in, 129–130, 132; steady growth business situations in, 124; U.S. government support of, 123, 125–126, 130, 195; vision quest business situations in, 127–129, 133. *See also* Business situations, common

Alexander, R. C., 159

Anderson, H., 154

Apple Computer, 9, 27, 157–164

The Art of the Long View (Schwartz), 15

"As We May Think" (Bush), 157

Assessment methodology. *See* Business situation assessment methodology

Atansoff, J. V., 142–143

Automobile industry, 115–122; commodity trap business situations in, 121; consolidation business situations in, 116, 120; crossing the chasm business situations in, 116; crossover business situations in, 120–122, 133; evolution business situations in, 115–116, 122; limits to change in, 67–68; process business situations in, 120, 133; silent war business situations in, 120–122; steady growth business situations in, 116, 120, 122; vision quest business situations in, 116–117, 133. *See also* Business situations, common

B

Babbage, C., 135

Bacon, R., 122

Baker, S., 34

Barker, J. A., 41

Baye's Rule, 94–95

Before the Computer (Cortada), 135

Bell, G., 155

Benz, C., 115

Berkowitz, B. D., 179

"A Better Mousetrap for Defense Conversion" (Clark and Werner), 181

Billings, J. S., 138

Blenkinsop, J., 111

Boeing, W., 123

Boole, G., 135

Brain mental model, 61

Branching and pruning business story, 58–59

Brandt, R., 34, 166

Branscomb, L. M., 193–194